FUNCTIONAL

A High Performer's Guide to
Achieving Freedom from Alcohol

Rachel Mack Martin

Copyright © 2025 by Rachel Mack Martin

ISBN

All rights reserved. No part of this publication may be reproduced, stored in a retrieval system, or transmitted in any form, or by any means, electronic, mechanical, photocopying, recording, or otherwise without the prior permission in writing of the copyright holder, nor be otherwise circulated in any form or binding or cover other than the one with which it was originally published, without a similar condition being imposed on the subsequent publisher.

The author is not a physician, and nothing in this book should be construed as medical advice.

Interior layout by Daiana Marchesi

FUNCTIONAL

Dedication

For everyone in the Rooms

"Once we have spoken our saddest story, we can be free of it."

— Taylor Swift

Contents

Author's Note ... xiii

Part I: What Does Functional Alcohol Use Disorder Look Like ... 1

The 3 a.m. Spiral ... 3
My Life Before Drinking Was a Problem ... 7
The Five Subtypes of Alcoholism and Gray Area Drinking ... 14
Rock Bottoms, Convincers, and Worries ... 20
Alcohol IS a Drug ... 27
Societal Pressures ... 32
Moderation and Taking a Break ... 37
Am I an Alcoholic? ... 39
Moderation Management ... 41

Functional Part II: Advice and Helpful Tips ... 47

Develop a Plan ... 49
Commit to 30 Days of Not Drinking ... 51
Just Do This One Thing ... 55
Get It Out of Your House ... 59
Tapering and Detox ... 62
Making Friends in Sobriety and Sober Communities ... 65
Join a Group ... 67
Follow: Social Media ... 69
Lead and Step Out ... 71
Deal With Your REAL Problem ... 73
Write a Breakup Letter to Your Substance ... 75

Date Yourself: #Selfcare That Is Real	78
"Who Am I Exercises?"	81
Tips for Going Out	84
Keep It Front and Center: Family Pictures, Affirmations, Talismans, and Tattoos	90
Cravings, Urges, and the Law of Substitution	95
Give Yourself Lots of Rest and Support	100
Time	101
What Do I Tell the PEOPLE?	103
Be Proactive and Tell Those You Care About	105
Pick a Phrase	106
Beyond Your Close Friends or Spouse, It Is Likely That No One Cares	108
The Art of the Pivot	110
Be Physical: Move Your Body	111
Journaling and *The Artist's Way*	114
One Day at a Time	116
Hit the Pillow Sober	118
Counting Time	120
Sponsors, Therapists, Coaches, and Mentors	123
AA Sponsors	125
Therapists and Recovery Coaches	128
Sober Role Models	130

Part III: Deeper Dives on Key Topics — 133

Sobriety in Days and What to Expect in Early Sobriety	135
My AA Experience	148

Being Out as Sober/Alcohol-Free: It Is YOUR Choice	156
Spouses, Partners, and Significant Others	162
Friend Groups	167
Slips and Relapses	170
Pain	176
Final Chapter: Contrast Your Drinking Self with Your Alcohol-Free Self	179

Recommended Resources 185

Author's Note

Confession: I never wanted to write this book publicly. I never wanted to write a book like this because I was embarrassed about my problems with alcohol. I was ashamed of how much I drank, how much money I spent, all the hangovers I had, and how I could not stop doing this damage to myself as a daily drinker.

I also worried that coming forward and authoring a book about my deepest and darkest struggle could hurt me professionally, especially as a woman.

My problem did not make any sense. On the one hand, I was successful in corporate America as a product manager and now a director with several licenses in my field and even an MBA. I had a husband, a nice home, and cute pets. I had put in the effort to build a functional life, and it was working. On the other hand, I counted down to 5 p.m. when I could walk in the door of my house, uncork a bottle, and pour a glass of wine, then another, and another, and proceed to get blotto. After I finally became alcohol-free and could sit back and assess my previous life, I discovered there are actually a lot of people like me. I call us the "Functionals."

The "Functionals" can be the moms who send our kids off to school every day. We manage multiple staff, and we are good employees. We run half-marathons on the weekends. We are lawyers, nurses, architects, and stay-at-home parents with three kids. We have Instagram-worthy lives, but we have a wine glass that can never seem to be full enough at the end of the day, the time when we let ourselves start drinking. This glass might as well be bottomless. We work hard to hide our habit from the world. We might have a few embarrassing incidents (I mean, who doesn't), but we believe we have it under control. Still, there is this nagging thought in the back of our minds that drinking is taking over our lives. We don't want to count down every day to 4 or 5 p.m. when it is finally wine o'clock. We want to be present for our kids and read them bedtime stories. We want to wake up fresh and without a hangover. We want to be in charge of our impulses and not need that drink at the end of the day.

But our days are hard, we are high performers, and people depend on us. The boss needs that last-minute report, and we have to work late to deliver it. The work assignment we're managing is taking longer and costs more than originally projected, and we are summoned by leadership to explain the status and present a turnaround plan to bring it to completion. The kids acted out in school, and we've been called into the principal's office. Our aging parents needed our help AGAIN to manage their increasingly challenging life. Really, is it any surprise that we *need* that glass—or more—for relief at the end of a stressful day?

Part I:
What Does Functional Alcohol Use Disorder Look Like

The 3 a.m. Spiral

It's 3 a.m. and I wake up anxiously as I do EVERY. SINGLE. NIGHT. My Egyptian cotton pillow is damp with sweat, my long, highlighted hair in tangles again from tossing and turning. Last night, I drank too much again, and all I can remember is popping the cork off the second bottle of chardonnay and not much after that. Did my husband give me the "you are drinking too much again" look? Did I stumble up our very steep flight of stairs to our bedroom before I passed out? What did I say to him? I knew I was a responsible person: I started drinking only after I came home from a full day at work. I always made dinner, and it usually had healthy and balanced servings of protein, carbs, and vegetables. I always made us eat together at the kitchen island to connect and discuss our day like civilized citizens—no meals scarfed down in front of the TV. I cleaned up the kitchen and ran the dishwasher and neatly packed away any leftovers for lunch the next day. For sure, the animals were fed before I got pleasantly bombed for the night.

My 3 a.m., anxious thoughts always fill me with shame, especially as I often cannot remember what I did the night before. I would learn years later that Chinese medicine says if you are active at 3 a.m., this could point to

Functional

liver issues. For a while, I've been trying to moderate my drinking and stick to one to two glasses of wine a night. But most of the time I am failing and drinking much, much more. Eventually I will discover that not having enough alcohol can be harder to deal with than not having any at all. I know that my husband, who rarely drinks, is growing increasingly disappointed with me and my behavior, even though I am continuing to do well at my high-paying job, running our house, and making dinner. One particular night, he tells me, with annoyance, that I am "repeating myself again." I feel intensely embarrassed—and perplexed that I do not recall having said something previously. Was I so blacked out that I couldn't remember what I'd said?

I lie there next to my soundly sleeping husband until about 4:15 a.m. My tongue touches my teeth, and they feel filmy. I already knew I didn't brush my teeth the night before again, causing me to have dog breath. Heck, I probably have mascara all over my pillowcase as well, because I didn't wash off my makeup. *Damn. I promised myself I wouldn't drink yesterday. I will do better today. I have a new resolution.*

So, I get out of bed, go downstairs and drink two precious cups of coffee to feel like a human again and get going with my day. Some mornings, I even force myself to go on a thirty-minute timed run through our housing development. I wave happily to the other, early morning neighbors who are "up and at 'em" with me by running like me or walking their dogs. My neighbors and I look at each other in recognition that we are high performers and positive contributors to society. After all, we start our day strong! I stare at them, a little too long, and I wonder if they're playing double agent, too, and like me are secretly hungover.

Come on. I can't be "that bad," right? True alcoholics don't wake up early and run before they go to a middle management, full-time job. My makeup is professional and precise, and I look perfectly put together with my

The 3 a.m. Spiral

Ann Taylor, properly proportioned ironed blouse and dress pants and matching jewelry. My head may be throbbing, but my hair is not out of place. And after all, I rationalize, I *need* to drink because my job is stressful and demanding. I must perform well, and drinking helps me handle the pressure.

Sometimes I stare at my reflection in the mirror. *Am I the only one noticing these changes?* Can anyone else tell that my eyes are puffy, and I slept poorly again? Sometimes I take pictures of myself after a night of drinking and compare them with pictures before I started having a problem. I do know there was a *before*. Is it just because I was so much younger, or do I really look this old and hollow now that I drink every day? My once blue eyes seem gray—dead and lackluster—the telltale sign of a heavy drinker. My complexion seems even red and inflamed, and I have a weird rash on my chest that never goes away no matter what magic skin product I try. Even my hair is drier and frizzier.

I may be able to mask the physical symptoms, but the shame is gutting me. The shame feels worse and worse, and it twists me in knots. The persistent 3 a.m. anxiety is dark, crippling, and I long for a time when I did not have it. My work life has always been stressful. But I cannot remember the timeline anymore: Did the 3 a.m. wake-ups come before I started drinking more—or after? Did I start drinking more because I was anxious, or have I grown more anxious because I am drinking? I think back to a time when I did not drink, when I felt less conflicted and more confident. More at peace. I remember feeling excited to embrace the day. Mornings were my favorite, instead of the nighttime when I could drink wine. I've always been a good problem solver and prided myself on addressing issues head-on. I know I must stop. What I don't know is how.

The above scenario describes my daily inner dialogue when I was drinking. Have you ever woken up in the middle of the night with anxiety like me? Do

Functional

you have conversations with people after you drink that you do not remember? Do you have frequent hangovers or feel like death the next morning after you drink? Do you rationalize your drinking and its impact on your life because you still go to work, pay bills, and get the kids to school? Because you are still ... functional?

My Life Before Drinking Was a Problem

My family was always a drinking family. My dad would come home and have beers after a hard day at work. My holidays would always involve aunts, uncles, and cousins with drinks in their hands. It all seemed very natural. Birthdays, baptisms, Easter, and Christmas dinners required drinks, because these were celebratory occasions. I did not think that my family was boozy; this was just what everyone did. When I met my husband's family, I saw them with a little skepticism and curiosity, as they rarely if ever drank. My husband's mother was a recovering alcoholic and attended A.A. His family holidays never included and still do not include alcohol, even after his mother's death. When I was still drinking, it felt downright unnatural and unhospitable to entertain family for the holidays without offering wine or beer to guests.

My mom was a devout Catholic who lived a highly structured life. My sisters and I were sent to private Catholic schools, and we prayed before meals and went to church every Sunday. I was the oldest daughter of three girls, and I understood at an early age that I was to set the example for my sisters. I was a "rule follower" and did not act up in school or at home. I

Functional

always completed my homework and was frequently at the top of my class academically. My mom was also rigid about our TV usage and limited my sisters and me to watching only *Scooby-Doo* when we came home from school. While TV time was monitored, we could check out as many books as we wanted from the local public library. I aggressively read all the books I could get my hands on, and both my reading level and mind expanded. I remember teachers telling me I sounded older than I was, and I believe that books featuring main characters with different perspectives enabled me to see the world with more maturity and complexity. While I did well in math and social sciences, my favorite class was English literature, and I was always, always reading.

When I was younger, despite my family's normalization of alcohol, I had a bad impression of people who drank heavily. I didn't like excessive drinkers with their loud voices and sloppy, slurring words. When I first tried drinking, I was around twelve; I remember not liking the taste or the strong smell. In fact, unlike so many people who have issues with alcohol from their first sip, I purposely stayed away from drinking in high school and rarely drank in college. I was too busy being an overachiever. Being in the top 5 percent of my peers academically, I went on to participate in a postsecondary program, where I completed university credits while still in high school. I ran track and cross-country. In college, I was an honor roll scholar and graduated early. All through college, I studied hard and worked at part-time jobs to pay my way, since my family did not finance my college education. Between a full course load and work, alcohol had no place in my life. This pattern would change, however, when I began my career in finance.

My major was English literature, and I had plans to become a high school English teacher. In my state, the requirements for my teaching license were four years of undergraduate study in English and a master's in education. The free university credits I'd accumulated while in high school knocked out a little over a year of college, but the remaining time, I paid for myself, partly through low-interest Plus loans my parents took out on which I made the payments. After working part-time while handling a full course load, even picking up extra shifts over breaks because I needed the money, I was exhausted and nearly broke. My plan was to work for about a year to be able to afford my master's program in education. Near graduation, I saw an ad in the local paper. "Are you a recent college graduate? Are you good at test taking?" It turned out to be an ad for a financial services company, and I would need to take a Series 6 license, which allowed me to discuss/solicit annuities and mutual funds. I could not have told you what an annuity or mutual fund was then, but I would be an associate for a large financial services firm, which I knew would pay way more than my physically demanding waitressing job.

Now, I do not have a network or even any connections in financial services or business, no family members or people I knew whose occupations were financial advisors, traders, or even businesspeople. My family had professions such as postal workers, nurses, and teachers. It really was up to me to succeed and build my professional network from the ground up. I did this in my twenties over happy hours or drinks with colleagues, and I learned that this was how business was conducted. My drink of choice was wine, which I viewed as different from beer, which seemed like a working-class, masculine drink. Wine was sophisticated and the signature drink of a professional female. I mostly drank whites, because I did not like the stain red wine made on my lips and teeth. Also, as I drank and networked more, my income and position increased.

Within a year of being at my company, it was obvious I would make far more money than an English teacher, so I never went back for that master's in education to become one. As I moved up the ranks in my job, I studied investments and voraciously read everything I

Functional

could about fixed income. I became a bond trader (a job I did for twelve years), and drinking was just "good business" and a necessary way to connect professionally. In addition, I was acutely aware that as a woman, I was a minority in my profession. I rarely met another woman trader, and women were almost surely under 15 percent of the overall trading personnel, especially in bonds. Drinking with colleagues was a professional asset, a tool that helped me participate and feel a sense of belonging with the guys.

If you ask me when drinking became a problem for me, I can tell you with certainty that 2007 and 2008 were distinct inflection points. Many people will remember that time as the housing bubble crash or the Great Financial Crisis. Home prices plummeted, financial markets were jolted, and many people lost their jobs. At the time, I was working as a bond trader. Bonds are an investment product that consumers flock to in times of safety, but some of the products I traded became stressed or ceased working as designed in a credit crunch. Bear Stearns and Lehman Brothers, two established financial service firms, went out of business overnight, causing dark ripples of scarcity and uncertainty in the bond market. One of our products became illiquid virtually overnight, and investors who needed their money could not get out. Advisors would call me daily and hound me for information, even though I had no answers. Their large, high-net-worth clients and institutions had millions of dollars that were impacted. Certain bonds were considered stable as cash, and for years investors would receive a small yield above cash with the ability to go in and out of auction with their bonds each week. For over seven years before the crisis, I would trade in and out of these securities on behalf of my advisors seamlessly and yet, overnight everyone was stuck—and panicked. Each night I would come home after talking to advisors who were tired and defeated, some with retiree clients dependent on this income stream, and I had no real alternatives to help them.

So, I would have a drink.

And maybe another.

After all, the world was falling apart.

So why not?

I remember my husband noticing my new habit and saying, "Every night when you come home now, you pour yourself a glass of wine first thing when you walk through the door." And that was what he saw. What he didn't see was that during the day, I would have to participate in legal discussions and arbitration hearings with our regulators. I remember receiving an email of encouragement and thanks from our CEO for the hearings and speaking on behalf of our company. I had a lot of people breathing down my neck, a lot of people to answer to. Management was watching, and my job was on the line. The stress was unbelievable. One bond trader in town with whom I traded would end up taking his own life. It would take nearly a year, but my company eventually offered clients rescission and an offer to buy them out of their illiquid positions, which was a relief.

Though I handled my work situation well, I felt trapped during the tumultuous years of 2007–2008. I then reported to another woman who viewed me as competition and went out of her way to make my daily life hell, even though my performance on paper was stellar. She was one of the meanest and most diabolical bosses I have ever had. If the economy had been normal, I could have left and found another position. But everything was frozen, especially in finance. There was no way I could leave and find another job making six figures, especially in the Midwest. My husband and I had just built our dream home, financially tethering me to my toxic work environment. In addition, the job market was horrible. It was not as if I could find another job making six figures,

Functional

because there were no jobs available during the Great Financial Crisis. Quickly, the glass of wine became two, then three, and then even more. Admittedly, I just kept up the wine habit, even after my work situation changed. Over time, drinking just became an established daily habit.

Even though problematic drinking began, I always performed. I would get up every morning to exercise before work, then work all day. I would stay late or participate in business dinners and happy hours. I was *functioning*. By many people's standards, I was highly functioning. I had all the external boxes checked. Married to a good husband: check. Bond trader in a competitive, all-male field: check. Pursuance and completion of a master's in business: check. A new, beautiful home with gorgeous hardwood floors: check. Two adorable Lab mix dogs: check. Fit body that ran distant races for fun: check. I checked all these boxes, and yet I was steadily and progressively drinking myself into oblivion or sleep every single night. At my height of drinking, I was drinking two bottles of wine daily and CHECKING out.

There is this false perception of addiction. The more I spend time in recovery rooms, the more I view addiction as a surprisingly normal coping mechanism. Many people have work stress like I did that starts a bad habit that has the potential to become an addiction. But at what point does it become dangerous and uncontrollable?

Now, I can see that this time in my life was incredibly stressful and lonely. Years later, I would recognize that a better solution would have been therapy. At that time, though, I did not see that as a solution because I was dealing with the work issue in what seemed to me a normal way. I would attend a work meeting that was stressful, and people would joke about going home and "having a drink over that one" or talk about drinking as a form of stress relief. What are a few drinks when you consider all the stress that we have?

Another part of my high-functioning drinking was the ability to stop when appropriate in public. I was never comfortable drinking more than two glasses of wine when out in the wo rld. I recognized that one drink relaxed and enlivened me instantly—and that was good. I would then have one more drink that I stretched out for the rest of the night. I really frowned on people who were noticeably intoxicated. That said, I knew I would get in the car and drive home, where a full bottle of wine would be waiting for me to finish it.

Was your upbringing similar? Does your family drink or celebrate milestones with alcohol? Did you have immense success academically or perform well at sports? Do you have a respectable job and are you respected in your profession? Are you a good mother or father and active in your kids' lives? Can you perform publicly and complete difficult tasks, yet you struggle with alcohol and are finding it more difficult to control your drinking? If so, you may be a Functional like me.

The Five Subtypes of Alcoholism and Gray Area Drinking

When I began going to AA meetings, I heard a lot of crazy stories from alcoholics. Things like getting children taken away, jail time, divorces, job losses, and home foreclosures.

That is not my story.

I did not have those problems.

What I did have in common with the people at those meetings was a drinking problem. I used to view these drastic outcomes that did not define my life as a rationale for why I could keep drinking. After all, if I could still maintain a functional life while drinking, why stop? I did not really understand myself until I learned about the five subtypes of alcoholics from the National Institute on Alcohol Abuse and Alcoholism (Source: 5 Types of Alcoholics: What Are the Subtypes of Alcoholics? alcohol.org). *Note: I truly hate the term alcoholic. "Alcoholic" is not a recognized medical term, but these subtypes of alcoholics were published in 2015, and that was the terminology. I found the categorization so helpful that I wrote this book based on the "Functional" subtype.*

Here, adapted from NIAAA, are the subtypes of alcoholics:

1. **Young Adult:** Experience compulsive behaviors around twenty years old. Have fewer occasions during an average week in which they drink but tend to binge drink on these occasions. Thirty-two percent of people with an alcohol use disorder fall into this category.

2. **Young Antisocial:** Defined by having antisocial personality disorder leading them to begin drinking in adolescence, around age fifteen on average. Twenty-one percent of people with an alcohol use disorder fall in this category.

3. **Functional:** Have higher income, more education, and stable relationships compared to other adults struggling with alcohol use disorder. Tend to binge drink, on average, every other day. Nineteen percent of people with an alcohol use disorder fall into this category.

4. **Intermediate Familial:** About half have close family members who abused alcohol. In response to family stress, these individuals typically began drinking around age seventeen. Nineteen percent of people with an alcohol use disorder fall into this category.

5. **Chronic Severe:** Most of the individuals in this group are male, with a high divorce rate and the highest rates of attendance at inpatient programs as well as polydrug abuse. Nine percent of people with an alcohol use disorder fall into this category.

The "Functionals" as I will continue to refer to myself and others in this category look normal. We pay taxes and mortgages. We maintain and even thrive in jobs.

According to the book *Understanding the High-functioning Alcoholic: Professional Views and Personal Insights* by Sarah Allen Benton, there are other characteristics of this subtype, such as "tending to restrict their use

Functional

and abuse to specific situations or times" or "tend[ing] to minimize the problems associated with their abuse of alcohol." I know that I would never have drunk during work, and many times I would never drink if I knew I needed to drive somewhere. In addition, I used to brush off how terrible my hangovers or gut issues were from my drinking. I wasn't happy with it, but I felt I could handle it. Another characteristic is that this group may have a spouse, family member, or administrator who may "cover" for them if they are drunk or hungover. Due to their education and professionalism, this type of covering may be necessary to keep jobs or the family intact, especially if Functional is a main provider.

Frankly, I see more functional alcohol use disorder examples than the stereotypical homeless guy under the bridge. Functionals are everywhere. They live highly productive daily lives but drink heavily at night and on weekends. Functionals know on some level their drinking isn't good. But it is no surprise that they question if they are "bad enough" to stop drinking—and rationalize the answer.

Being a Functional is confusing, because when comparing yourself to people who are worse, you minimize your problem with alcohol. When I attend meetings or interact with other people with alcohol use disorder, I often hear terrible stories of rock-bottom moments—DUIs, divorces, job terminations, etc. These consequences for drinking can be minimized depending on your socioeconomic status. For example, as a professional woman with no children, I would be less likely to drive dependent kids and more likely to pay for an Uber if I thought that there was a likelihood that I was drinking. That would improve my chances of not obtaining a DUI. I also would preplan a hotel room if I knew that I would be out drinking, which may not be on everyone's budget. I also cared greatly about my employment and the consequences related to a job, so that kept me from having some issues.

Sometimes, when I interact with people in recovery, I realize that there are people who never had good habits in place prior to drinking. For various reasons, they are more comfortable with chaos than I ever would be. That is the other thing about people with an alcohol problem. The thing we all have in common is that we drink too much. Other than that, those who struggle with drinking can look quite different from each other. Some people tell me that they knew they were a problem drinker from the first sip of liquor and could never control their drinking. People will tell me that they honestly did not know that would be their progression. My experience was different, however, and many high-functioning or functional subtypes do not share that experience. We may drink more or drink longer than some, until embarrassing moments become more frequent and prompt an examination of consciousness or motivation to change.

Gray Area Drinking

There is another interesting category close to mine that bears discussing. This category is not recognized by doctors or treatment centers, but it is observable in the sober sphere and called "gray area drinking." I first heard about it from a woman named Jolene Park who talked about her history of stopping and starting drinking. When she drank, she would drink most nights, but no one would call her an alcoholic, because she could stop or take breaks. She called this drinking "gray area drinking," defined as "the kind of drinking where there's no rock bottom, but you drink as a way to manage anxiety and then regret how much and how often you drink" (Source: Gray Area Drinking | ted.com).

Gray area drinkers may start and stop drinking. They may take months off drinking. They likely do not drink every day. They recognize that drinking is not serving them, and they question their drinking a lot because it doesn't feel good, but they do not see themselves as suffering

Functional

from alcoholism nor does the world view them in that light. It would never occur to a gray area drinker to go to an AA meeting, for example. Their behavior would not be "bad enough," yet they still do not like their relationship with alcohol.

There are many similarities between gray area drinking and high-functioning alcoholism. While I see my specific category as functional alcohol use disorder, because I did not feel like I could stop and it was impacting my life, I recognize that prior to being in that box, I had a period of gray area drinking. I could not have expressed this at the time, and I was not aware of the gray area category. I find it helpful though, because knowing about it would have enabled me to understand the nature of my problem as I examined myself. As Jolene says, "Grey area drinking is extremely common," which is why it is relevant to bring up. In my opinion, gray area drinkers recognize that something does not work with their drinking. Maybe they feel like they drink too much. Maybe they feel they use alcohol to manage anxiety and do not like their dependence. Maybe, they look around, see everyone drinking, and wonder if they are drinking differently.

While labels like "functional "or "gray area drinking" were helpful for me to define myself and see myself for what I was, they may not be your thing now or in the future. It was difficult for me to wrap my head around my problem, because I looked different from what I thought someone with an alcohol problem looked like. Learning about types of alcohol problems that looked like mine was extremely helpful.

When I label myself to the outside world now, I like to say that I am "alcohol-free." I have not drunk alcohol in over six years. I never say alcoholic. I rarely say sober. We would not say that a person who quits cigarettes is a "cigarette-aholic" for the rest of their lives. When wait staff ask me what I'd like to drink at a restaurant, I do not announce to a perfect stranger that "I am an alcoholic and can't drink." This seems too personal and, in a way, self-shaming. I simply tell the server that I am alcohol-free and ask about their NA (nonalcoholic) options. I find this the easiest way to navigate the inevitable question of what I'll be drinking.

When I do have a conversation with someone who may have a problem similar to mine, or if I feel like explaining to someone how my life became so much better, identifying myself as having functional alcohol use disorder defines exactly where I was before I became alcohol-free.

How do you feel when you read the subtypes? Do you resonate with living a double, secret agent life? Do you see similarities to yourself as a Functional or a gray area drinker? Is there a different term or description that you would use to describe how you drink?

Rock Bottoms, Convincers, and Worries

Sometimes, I meet people who either stop drinking or want to stop drinking because they experience a rock-bottom moment when something terrible happens and they know they must quit. A mom in long-term recovery told me she knew she could no longer deny drinking was a problem when she was pulled over for drunk driving with her kids in the car. She remembered her daughter watching from the back seat with frightened, wide eyes as she had to get out and perform a sobriety test in front of a police officer. For her, this was the defining rock-bottom moment when it became undeniable that her drinking was impacting others. Not only that, but her drinking also had become a crime and a real threat to her family's safety. She knew that she had to stop immediately.

I did not have a rock-bottom moment. I did, however, have plenty of "convincing moments" that started to stack up, which when combined brought me to the conclusion that alcohol was not working in my life anymore. I read a book early in sobriety called *The Unexpected Joy of Being Sober* by Catherine Gray, and in it she discusses what she calls "Convincers." Convincers are a series of moments in your life when you face a defining moment of truth. They shine a light on issues you may not want to acknowledge. Below, I list these convincers from my own experiences when I could no longer pretend or delude myself that nothing was wrong with how I was living.

Convincer #1: Two years before I became sober, my husband initiated a conversation with me about my drinking. It was a weekend, and I had started with wine at noon and was in bed at 2 p.m. because I needed a nap to sleep it off. My husband came into our bedroom quietly, sat down on the side of the bed, and I woke up. He did not even preface the conversation with small talk. In a deliberate voice with evident frustration he asked, "Rachel, why am I not enough? Why do you need the wine?" I did not expect the question and could not even explain why wine had become so important to me. I stared up at my husband and saw his pretty blue eyes shaded with sadness and recognized that I had a nearly flawless soulmate in front of me asking me why he wasn't as important as a stupid glass of fermented grape juice. This was the man who had built me a dream home with his two hands. This was my supportive husband who listened to all my dreams and aspirations, who loved my family, and who was what society would call "a good guy." Here he was, and I could not answer him. His question was valid. I just did not know how to respond.

I did not stop drinking then, but I thought a lot about his words long after he'd spoken them to me. Slowly, my mind began to reframe things. While his question hadn't been accusatory, I realized that *I* was the one who was screwing things up by putting something else—by putting drinking—ahead of my most important relationship.

Convincer #2: I attended a bonfire hosted by a woman in our neighborhood. At the time, I was living in a new house in a well-appointed development. I was a career-focused woman and the only one in the development who was not a mother. I attended the bonfire because I did know some of the women there and thought they were friendly. I was looking forward to

Functional

it and had even bought a cute pair of campfire boots to wear. After my first hour, it was obvious that all the conversation would center around everyone's kids. I felt out of place, but stuck since I did not want to be the first to leave. So, out of boredom and feeling like I didn't fit in, I ended up drinking more wine than was socially acceptable. Later that night, I drove my car home, which was one block away from the campfire. When I woke up the next day, I felt miserable. I felt even worse when I saw my new boots sprawled by the side of the bed with their soles melting. *How did that happen?* I don't remember putting my feet so close to the fire that it melted my boots! One of the heels was so warped that I didn't even know how I would have properly walked in it. I stubbornly decided to get out of bed, because I was a huge exerciser and even hungover, I went on a run. The neighbor who hosted the party saw me run by her house and snickered, "How are you feeling this morning?" I gulped and realized I must have been more visibly intoxicated than I allowed myself in public. Later I heard from another lady who was more tactful. She took me aside and said I'd gotten in my car and driven over a curb, after which she and another neighbor had watched me swerve down the block, then park and go into my house. She said she made sure I got home.

This was embarrassing for me because I could not remember much about it, and I hated looking stupid in public. After that night, I never drank that way around those neighbors again. That said, it still never made me stop.

Convincer #3: It is 5:30 in the morning, and I am getting ready for work in our kitchen, packing lunches as if nothing is wrong and it's an ordinary morning. Earlier, I woke up at 2 a.m. and I am shaking. I'd picked myself up out of my bed, from next to my sleeping husband, to go downstairs and drink a few glasses of wine until I felt better. The shaking stopped, and I went back to bed as if nothing had happened. Then, like a good wife, I wake up when the alarm goes off and start my day with coffee as I pack our lunches for work. My husband knows something is off and asks, "Are you still drunk?" as he stares hard at me. "No," I say, refusing to meet his eyes.

I go back to sleep when he leaves. I have a normal-grade hangover. That morning, I had planned a dermatologist appointment for an odd-looking mole. But my drunk mind now tells me this mole is no big deal. I leave a voicemail for the dermatologist, in which I probably sound drunk, and go back to sleep. I wake up again at 10 a.m. and go to work in the afternoon.

A week later, my husband and I talked about that morning. I told him I did not go to work until later in the day after I had slept, and he feels relieved about my answer. I am still a good member of society, still in control, not embarrassing myself, not jeopardizing work.

Convincer #4: I went out with a friend to see a movie. The organizer ended up buying tickets to the wrong theater, so we went out for drinks instead. I came home late and needed to keep drinking when I got home. The next morning, my husband was irate and noticeably upset. "If you get whiskey plates on our vehicles," he told me, "I'm leaving you." This was not the questioning, sad husband who had quietly asked me before why he was not enough. This was a man drawing the line and telling me he would no longer tolerate the risk my drinking presented. Now, for those who do not live in a state that has "whiskey plate laws," I will explain. Minnesota will give you special license plates that replace your regular license plates and will start with the letter "W." They are given after a "DWI" conviction and are required for your vehicle and anyone else in your household on your insurance. These plates enable law enforcement to spot you more easily and subject you to more scrutiny if stopped. My husband's words amounted to an ultimatum that could ultimately lead to divorce. This conversation shook me. Of course, in my quick thinking at the time, I rationalized it and concluded that the solution was to Uber in the future instead of making the necessary changes in my behavior.

Functional

These convincers stacked up to present a reality about myself that I could not deny. I did not like these versions of Rachel, especially because I was an achiever, cared about what people thought of me, and placed great importance on my relationships, especially my marriage. These convincers nagged at me, and they pushed me to change.

Perhaps you do not have convincers, but you have worries instead. I describe worries as little, nagging, negative thoughts that plagued my mind and expanded, particularly when I drank or as a result of my drinking.

Here are some of my worries. Are any of these on your list?

1. **Driving drunk.** I always worried that when I drove, I had to pay attention not to be intoxicated enough to get pulled over and get a DWI. Many of my girlfriends had been pulled over: Some just received warnings and some ended up with a DWI. My friends who have received them are defensive or do not admit their part (unless they are in recovery).

2. **Being taken advantage of.** As women, we worry that we might be taken advantage of, assaulted, or raped while under the influence. Many women have gone home with a guy that they did not know that well and had something occur that was not consensual. Alcohol is present in 70 percent of rape cases. It makes women vulnerable, not powerful.

3. **Falling down the stairs and hurting myself.** My home has steep stairs that go from the main floor to the upstairs bedrooms. I used to walk up the stairs and worry that I would fall back. I have met women struggling to get sober, and they have the telltale marks of bruises they do not remember how they got. It turns out they fell. Stupidly, I remember all the times I wore cute heels and went out to some trendy bar or restaurant and fell—or almost fell—when I drank too much.

4. **Would I still be drunk when I had to perform?** Have you ever heard the story of the person who received a DWI in the morning on their way to work because they had been drunk the night before? I felt so hungover and out of it some mornings that I had difficulty remembering where I parked at the park and ride. Also, sometimes I would go to bed early (passing out), then wake up in the night and need more wine. I would drink to get myself back to sleep, then worry about being intoxicated in the morning when I had to be at work.

5. **Will I lose my keys, phone, or credit card?** I once left my credit card at a bar when I was out drinking. I have frantically searched for my phone in my purse, not realizing it had fallen into a pocket where I never would have put it sober. If you lose your credit card or phone, you can usually retrace your steps and check all the places you've been—unless you don't remember. It is highly embarrassing to explain to a restaurant or a family member that has to come and pick you up that you were out drinking and cannot remember what happened to something so critical.

6. **Would my drink be too high-proof, or would my food intake not be enough to settle the alcohol?** I always worried about my inebriation level. This is not a concern if you just have one drink, but most people will have more than one when they go out. I have been to restaurants where the server pours you more than a standard glass of wine or food portions are too small. If there wasn't enough food to absorb the alcohol, I would worry that I'd end up too intoxicated to drive. As a result, I would try spacing out drinks or drinking a glass of unsatisfying water between drinks, which just made me crabby.

7. **Would I be drunk and someone of importance see me?** I was out in the middle of nowhere at a Swedish restaurant by a vineyard an hour and a half away from the city where I work. At the vineyard, I tasted multiple samples plus a large glass of wine. I did have a designated driver. That

Functional

said, we all decided to go to the restaurant near the vineyard to get some food to temper all the wine we'd drunk. I saw my boss's boss, while I was at least three glasses deep. She joked that she was mortified to be out in sweatpants and hat hair, and she did not expect to see anyone she knew so far away. I looked cute in my winery wardrobe, but I was careful to say only a few words for fear of slurring them.

8. **Was I going to fall to a nonfunctional level?** As I drank more and had more hungover mornings, I began to imagine myself in a smaller home, without a husband, and without a job. Would I become a public drunk? The alcohol use disorder spectrum has a homeless guy at the end with a red, splotchy face and fingerless gloves who clutches his bottle with a death grip as he drinks outside in the cold, huddling over a fire in a barrel. The more you drink, the more this guy's fate seems likely in your future. I noticed my husband had grown sick of my daily drinking, and I started to worry he might actually leave me—and I would be alone. One morning I woke up still drunk and had the terrifying thought that I might not make it to work and that behavior like this would lead to losing my job. Even living in a nice suburb with an excellent job and education, you start to worry/wonder what a smaller apartment might look like or rationalize how being single might not be so bad. I used to wonder if feeling small and settling for much less was just a part of getting older. When you sober up, though, it becomes obvious that this is what addiction looks like—it hijacks your brain into accepting less so alcohol can take over your life.

When you read over these rock bottoms, convincers, and worries, do any of them resonate? Do you recall instances of drinking too much and doing something out of character? Have there been situations that you were embarrassed about? Have there been relationships of yours that have been impacted because of your drinking? Have you drunk and almost jeopardized a job or had a fight with an important person in your life?

Alcohol IS a Drug

"Why is it so damn difficult to moderate?!" I used to wonder as I would blow past my glass (or two) daily limit. For several years, I thought the answer was simply to drink less. If I could just stick to a glass a day of wine, or even just drink three to four times a week, that would be great. That would mean that I could control this thing. I could never consider stopping entirely. I mean, what was I going to do at weddings when they toasted to the happy couple or at happy hour when I was expected to drink for business? It seemed unfathomable to stop, yet moderation was its own hell. All the planning to only stick to one drink or control myself not to drink more, especially when I knew I had to drive. Frankly, it sucked, and I was not having fun.

For those of us who are Functionals, the inability to moderate feels like utter failure. I could not understand how I could achieve high grades, obtain industry licenses, be successful at my job, even complete home renovations ... but I could not moderate alcohol. The scary thing was that I really was never winning when it came to moderation. It grew increasingly difficult and sometimes I would just lose control, end up blacking out at home, then wake up at 3 a.m. full of shame. This

Functional

Groundhog Day of failing moderation decimated my confidence and crashed into my self-worth.

When I was trying to get better, at least initially I put the focus on myself. After all, I was failing. I was not moderating. It was me who was the problem.

When I stopped drinking, I began researching everything that I could about addiction and why I was the way I was. Even though I was relatively well-read and possessed a master's degree, I was not at all educated about alcohol. The only thing I knew for sure was that people who drank too much were bad and alcoholics. Alcoholics, however, were better than DRUG addicts. We know that meth, heroin, and crack are drugs. Alcoholism was something that could mysteriously happen to you, but drinking alcohol—as long as you didn't drink too much—was harmless overall, right?

To begin with, alcohol ACTUALLY is a drug and classified that way by the medical community. Alcohol is one of the most widely used addictive drugs in the world. Also, alcohol is EVERYWHERE. Alcohol is at most weddings, family celebrations, grocery stores, and nearly all restaurants. It is toxic, and people who try it for the first time can balk at its taste.

Below is a compilation of statistics about alcohol that I have found useful.

- The World Health Organization (WHO) has stated that "no level of alcohol consumption is safe for our health" (Source: No Level of Alcohol Consumption Is Safe for Our Health | who.int). Even a single drink is a net negative for the drinker regardless of whether you have a problem. Yes, even that glass of red wine with antioxidants is bad for you, and you would be better off having grapes than a glass filled with poison.

- The US Centers for Disease Control and Prevention estimated an annual average of 178,000 people die from alcohol-related causes such as motor vehicle crashes, alcohol poisoning, cancer, and cirrhosis, based on data from 2020 and 2021 (Source: Deaths from Excessive Alcohol Use, United States, 2016–2021 | cdc.gov). From 2016–2021, the number of deaths from alcohol-related causes jumped 29 percent due to the effects of the pandemic and isolation, which is also a startling statistic.

- "Drinking in moderation" is defined by the CDC as one drink or less in a day for women and two drinks or less in a day for men (cdc.gov). Now, I do not know about you, but I really cannot think of many people who would meet that definition of "moderate." I surely drank more than that even when I did not know that I had a problem, especially when the CDC defines a standard US drink size as twelve ounces of beer (5% alcohol content) or five ounces of wine (12% alcohol content).

- Drinking alcohol impacts your skin and complexion. Our skin is our largest organ, and it is no surprise that alcohol can make you look worse. Those who consume higher levels of alcohol can incur rashes, yellow skin, spider veins, and skin that appears red for no reason. Acne, rosacea, eczema, and psoriasis are also common (Source: Alcohol and Aging: Does Alcohol Use Make You Look Older? gracelandrecovery.com). In addition, it dehydrates your skin and causes wrinkles. We all have seen the pictures on Instagram where someone stops drinking and even after one to three months, their collagen levels improve and their skin glistens and looks noticeably younger (Source: Drinking Is Probably Aging You Much More Than You Realize | huffpost.com).

- One of our most necessary daily requirements in life is sleep. Even one glass of alcohol a day can negatively impact your sleep. For example, having two servings of alcohol per day for men or one serving per day for women will decrease sleep quality by 24% (Source: Alcohol and

Functional

Sleep | sleepfoundation.org). I know that I used alcohol to help me fall asleep, which absolutely can make you sleepy. That said, drinking to fall asleep builds tolerance, which will force you to consume more alcohol to get to sleep, which makes you have a worse quality of sleep. It is a terrible cycle.

- Alcohol WORSENS your mental health, especially depression and anxiety. As many as 80 percent of alcoholics report a series of sadness and depression (Source: Alcohol, Anxiety, and Depressive Disorders | nih.gov). I cannot tell you the number of people I have met who truly thought that they were mentally unwell who gave up drinking and felt so much better, then recognized it was actually the alcohol that was making them depressed (after all alcohol is a depressant). Similarly, your anxiety can lessen or go away after you stop drinking.

- There has been a concerted effort by alcohol companies to market their drug to women. It makes us fun and strong, and we can even drink with the boys. That said, alcohol can put everyone at more risk of sexually abusing another person or being abused. According to a campus sexual assault study created by the NCJRS, "43% of [...] sexual victimization incidents involved alcohol consumption by victims and 69% involved alcohol consumption by the perpetrator" (Source: How the Use of Alcohol Plays a Role in Sexual Assault | alcoholaddictioncenter.org).

- As I was completing edits for this book, the US Surgeon General finally issued a new advisory on the link between alcohol and cancer risk. The most quoted line from the advisory is that "Alcohol is a well-established, preventable cause of cancer responsible for about 100,000 cases of cancer and 20,000 cancer deaths annually in the United States—greater than the 13,500 alcohol-associated traffic crash fatalities per year in the US—yet the majority of Americans are unaware of this risk," said Surgeon General Dr. Vivek Murthy.

"This Advisory lays out steps we can all take to increase awareness of alcohol's cancer risk and minimize harm" (Source: U.S. Surgeon General Issues New Advisory on Link Between Alcohol and Cancer Risk | hhs.gov). Alcohol is a carcinogen and there are several cancers associated with drinking including head and neck cancer, esophageal cancer, liver and colorectal cancer, and breast cancer. Part of the Surgeon General's recommendation is to put a health warning label on alcohol-containing beverages to warn about cancer, especially because less than half of Americans actually understand that alcohol consumption increases your risk of cancer (Source: Alcohol and Cancer Risk 2024 | hhs.gov). I know that when I drank, I never, ever thought about wine causing cancer, because there were so many articles telling me that a little bit would actually benefit me. In hindsight, these articles were probably created by the alcohol industry or people benefiting from alcohol consumption.

Based on all these statistics and more I did not cite, we really must stand back and ask ourselves if alcohol is an innocent and harmless drug and if we really should even risk drinking at all?

One question that I sometimes think about is if alcohol were "discovered" today, would it be legal? Would we have a standard food label like we have on all products—even yogurt—that have calories disclosed? Would there be more warning labels? Would health and fitness advocates who focus on organic and vegetarian foods endorse this drug?

My message is this: It does not matter if you are "an alcoholic"; alcohol is BAD for EVERYONE.

What are your thoughts on alcohol? Do you think it is handled like an addictive drug? Have you noticed that people who use a lot of it or for a long period of time appear to be "less healthy"? Does hearing that it is a carcinogen cause you concern?

Societal Pressures

One of my favorite vintage chick flick TV shows is *Sex and the City*. In the series, witty Manhattan writer Carrie Bradshaw analyzes the difficulty of dating while clutching a Cosmopolitan in sophisticated stemware. As the quintessential single girl, Carrie ventures out to bars in her little black dresses to meet men and enjoys boozy brunches with her gal friends. Especially in my twenties and thirties, I've watched *Sex and the City* episodes over and over again. The show taught me about relationships, dating, friendship, and of course, drinking. The main beverage of choice is the famed Cosmo—featured in numerous scenes—as well as wine. My most beloved scenes feature Carrie, Miranda, Samantha, and Charlotte sitting at a table loaded with drinks discussing their disappointments.

For example, Carrie's main love interest, Mr. Big, has his engagement party at the Plaza—with his fiancée who is *not* Carrie. Later, Carrie and her girlfriends gather around the table in a crowded New York restaurant, and she asks why Mr. Big is marrying a plain, unexciting girl while Carrie is bright and beautiful with frizzy hair and yet all alone when it comes to love. Her vulnerable share asks the age-old question: "Why am I not enough?" Carrie's girlfriends soothe her broken heart with deep listening skills, sympathy, and of course another round of drinks. Alcohol is a natural part of the scene and embedded in their lives. In fact, there is so much drinking, that the Cosmo could be another character in the show.

Alcohol is ubiquitous. It is at every Christmas dinner, where there's wine on the table and rum in the eggnog, and at every wedding reception when we clink champagne glasses to celebrate the new couple. Taking your first drink is a rite of passage that establishes you as an adult. It is customary and friendly to "meet for drinks" and to offer a guest a drink when they come to your home. Alcohol is almost always involved with meeting your significant other—in a bar, at a party, or on a date set up online. No one stops to question this kind of drinking.

In countries such as the US, you must be twenty-one years old to drink legally. But young people first begin experimenting with drinking in high school, or even earlier, by attending parties with alcohol, often unsupervised. In college, spring break, frat parties, and campus bars cater to the habit. It is normal to drink and an eventual and expected adult activity. I have spoken with mothers who want to prepare their daughters for college and increase their tolerance for alcohol by having them drink at home safely before heading off to school and indulging in rowdy nights. After all, these mothers rationalize, on the inevitable long nights of beer chugging and drinking games, inexperience and rapid inebriation would embarrass their children or worse, put them in a potentially compromising situation with boys. Why not just teach them to drink and keep them safe?

As we move into our mid-twenties and young adulthood, drinking at bars and happy hours with our coworkers is a normal, seemingly essential part of networking, meeting romantic partners, and hanging out with friends. The company I work for has a Young Professional employee

Functional

group that sponsors events for our younger employees, and nearly all are after 4 p.m. and involve a happy hour. First dates nearly always involve meeting for a drink, and even workout events like yoga or dog meetups take place at breweries. Alcohol consumption is a normalized component of society.

Into my twenties and thirties, happy hours continued as a natural way to network, make business connections, and find out what people "really felt" about their team or leader after they'd been loosened up by a few drinks. When a coworker moved to a different department or the team would celebrate a project completion, going out for drinks was standard operating procedure. It was not a "requirement of the job," but most professionals know that to thrive within a company, they need to interact with their coworkers, subordinates, or bosses socially. When I was three or four years out of college, I attended a work celebration and spoke to a coworker who had left my department and told me that the new group they were going to paid more, had less "grunt work," and the "leadership was cool." Of course, that colleague then recommended me for an open position, and I slid easily into a role I would have never known about if I hadn't attended the happy hour. Alcohol was a good thing. Alcohol connected me to job opportunities.

As I grew older, the happy hours continued and expanded into business dinners. Instead of the cheap beer, "two for one" specials, and inexpensive business outfits that dominated my early twenties, now bottles of nice wine were shared around the table at dinner as I sat and chatted in my fitted, little black dresses from Nordstrom. It was customary to drag out these networking affairs with pre-dinner and after-dinner drinks. Throughout the meal, competitive intelligence, industry job changes, and strategy would be openly shared. I always viewed these experiences—and the drinking that went with them—as "part of the job." Of course, I would worry about how much I was drinking, especially if I knew that I had to drive home. For some annual events, I planned ahead and got a hotel room, so I wouldn't need to be sober enough to drive home and could more easily make the following early morning meeting or presentation. After all, I would hear in confidence that some people from my company had gotten pulled over and received a DWI. It was understandable! I mean, how else could you drink for four to five hours straight and be expected to pass a sobriety test?! I thought I was being responsible and demonstrating intelligent foresight by getting a room to pass out in after those power nights out. It never occurred to me that I could have just cut back on my drinking or even gone alcohol-free. I'm sure I was worried my colleagues would think I was strange, or think less of me, for not keeping up with their drinking.

When someone stops drinking or even just takes a break, their decision is questioned because drinking is so commonplace. If a younger woman passes up a drink, we are inevitably asked, "Are you pregnant?" or "Is there something important you need to be sharp for in the morning?" Even though alcohol is an addictive drug and damaging to our health, not drinking is seen as an odd choice that needs to be justified. Fortunately, as people become more educated about the dangers of alcohol as a drug, this questioning is diminishing. With so much societal pressure and even stigmatization of nondrinkers (even though alcohol abusers are the ones with a problem), is it any wonder we become so easily addicted? We go from an occasional beer or glass of wine to social drinking to heavy consumption and it seems like a natural, unavoidable progression. It is as if we wake up one day and think, "When did everyone around me start drinking so much and why am I now craving alcohol every day?!"

"Mommy" play dates, sports outings, and nights out with girlfriends may all involve drinking. A drink or two that happened only on weekends, can become a drink or two every night. Suddenly, we are caught up in an "acceptable" addiction.

Going back to *Sex and the City*, the ladies would eventually have to confront all those nights with Cosmos. In the spinoff, *And Just Like That*, which aired in 2021, we see Miranda ordering wine before noon and follow her journey of realizing she has a problem with alcohol. She orders sober-curious books online, starts attending AA meetings, and eventually gets sober. Of course, *Sex and the City* and *And Just Like That* are just TV shows and cannot actually dive into the hours of self-reflection and difficult mindset changes that occur in real life when you decide to remove alcohol from your life. That said, the twenty-something-year-old female in me who watched the first show with giddy excitement and wonder, really appreciated the result of all that drinking, which led to the consequence of Miranda becoming sober. All those boozy Manhattan scenes and marrying bartender Steve had the inevitable outcome of addiction. Just as I had initially watched the ladies perch on their pub stools with drinks in their hands, I watched them rally around Miranda with her nonalcoholic beverage. There was a kind of full-circle moment, and I appreciated the show's writers carrying Miranda's storyline through and addressing the effects of preventing alcohol use.

When did you first begin experimenting with drinking and what did that look like? What role does alcohol play in your own celebrations? If you remember your last family holiday like Easter, Christmas, or Thanksgiving, what alcohol—and how much—was served? What is your drink of choice (wine, beer, whiskey, etc.)? Do you work in an industry or job environment where it seems you're required to drink a lot? If you do have kids, do your activities and your socializing with parents include heavy drinking?

Moderation and Taking a Break

When I first thought about taking a break from alcohol, I was never thinking about it as FOREVER. To me, forever meant I would never connect at a business meal over drinks. FOREVER meant I would never enjoy family holidays, weddings, or any Saturday night again. I did not know how I would relate to people at work if we could not joke about how a 5 p.m. meeting conflicted with our evening drinking time. I thought if I stopped drinking for an extended period, I would lose my whole life as I knew it and be deprived of important opportunities at work and enjoyment of my leisure time. As it turns out, I was both right and wrong.

By this time, I was stacking up more and more convincers and worries. I wanted to be in the category where drinking was not impacting my job and my relationships. I wanted to feel good when I woke up in the morning. Yet, not drinking seemed like it would change my whole lifestyle and, in many ways, make things worse. As a successful Functional, I had built friendships around winery trips and networked through business events with an always-full glass of wine in my hand. I viewed alcohol as a tool I needed to be successful, and I worried that

Functional

my whole identity would crumble if I did not have it in my life. I knew on some level my drinking was bad, but was it bad enough to quit? And what would be the consequences?

Am I an Alcoholic?

I am going to tell you something directly. Once you start thinking you have a problem, you *have* a problem. If you are googling "How do you know if you are an alcoholic?" I will tell you right now with utter conviction: You have a problem with alcohol. You may have a *big* problem with alcohol. You may have a minor problem with alcohol, but you have a problem. You can choose to dig the hole deeper and make the problem larger and more difficult to get out of, or you can recognize that you are in a hole and need to get out.

I remember answering the questions I found on the AA website. Some of the questions were, "Have you ever decided to stop drinking for a week or so, but only lasted for a couple of days?" YES. "Have you ever switched from one kind of drink to another in hope that this would keep you from getting drunk?" YES. "Has your drinking caused trouble at home?" YES. Nearly every answer was YES. The question that absolutely scared me was, "Do you have blackouts?" and knowing the answer to that was YES gave me a wretched, embarrassing feeling.

When you're blacked out, you don't know you're blacked out. My husband would tell me things I did not remember happening the night before, such

Functional

as our cat doing something adorable and me taking a picture. I would smile and say, "Oh yes, I remember that." But I would be lying. I would then check my phone, and sure enough, there would be photographic evidence of a cat picture that I had no memory of taking the night before. As a person who took pride in my strong sense of responsibility, it killed me that I was doing things while I was unaware of my actions.

The yes answers added to the convincer list. Once I started understanding I had a problem, I did what any Functional or analytical person would do—I started researching intensively and reading up on the topic.

Sometimes when you start googling problems, you ask the wrong question. Let me explain. I wanted to "cut back" on drinking, not give it up. I wanted to *moderate*. I didn't see drinking as the problem—the issue was that I was just drinking *too much*. I found different books and information about moderation. I thought of solving my drinking problem as going on a diet focused on portion control. When we eat too much, we go on a diet. We count calories and keep track of how much we eat. I tried (and was sometimes successful) at only having one glass of wine a night. I was an "A" student and trained in using planning and willpower. I had built my whole life on it. If you are a Functional or high-functioning person, planning and willpower are tools for a successful life. They enabled me to graduate college in under four years and complete my MBA. They enabled me to run several distance races, including a marathon.

My husband and I built an entire home, mostly ourselves, with these same skills. They were the bedrock of how I operated my life, and I thought I could count on them to help me reduce my drinking.

Moderation Management

In my quest for moderation, I found an alcohol reduction program called Moderation Management. Moderation Management is like going on a diet and using an app to track eating and caloric intake. At the time that I was completing the program in earnestness, there was a board on the Internet with participants' names (you could list your real name or an alias) and a weekly tracking of how many drinks each person had during the week. An "ideal week" would be two to three days a week when you do not drink, followed by two to three days when you have only one or two drinks. The public board where you track your daily number of drinks encouraged honesty. Here are some examples of what I saw. John would not drink for twelve days, but on day thirteen, he would have *eleven* drinks. (How anyone can count eleven drinks is beyond my comprehension.) Next, Megan would start the week well. She would have one drink on Monday, two drinks on Tuesday, Wednesday would be zero, then Thursday would be five and her week would continue to slide.

At one point, Megan's drinking pattern closely resembled my own. When I reviewed those public boards with drinks tracked, no one was successful at maintaining one to two drinks at a time, including me.

Functional

There was a benefit, however. It helped me to clearly see that I could not meet a goal.

Now, back to the creator of Moderation Management. Her name was Audrey Kishline. Audrey went to rehab and looked around at all the alcoholics who had lost jobs, homes, and relationships. She saw she was clearly not one of them. She decided she was a "problem drinker" and not an alcoholic. She rejected the whole idea of alcoholism and decided to apply harm reduction techniques and cognitive behavioral therapy (CBT) tools to her drinking. This part of her story appeals to me, because I, too, separated myself from people who were "down-and-out" alcoholics as well. Like me, Audrey was high-functioning. She even authored a book in 1994 called *Moderation Management*, which put her on Oprah. (Such a Functional person's response to a problem: I will write a book.)

Though it seemed Audrey had her drinking under control, eventually she hit another vehicle, killing a twelve-year-old girl and her father. Audrey was driving the wrong way on the highway with a .26 blood alcohol level—more than three times the legal limit. She served three and a half years (of a four-and-a-half-year sentence) in prison, then returned to hard drinking after her release. When she died in her mother's home, many sources would confirm that she committed suicide, although her mother (understandably) has denied this claim.

While Audrey is just one example, I do believe her story sheds crucial light on moderation. I believe it is not possible to moderate an addictive drug, such as alcohol. Addicts cannot moderate heroin, meth, or cigarettes; why do we believe it is possible with alcohol?

There is also another breadcrumb I found in my searches. A person's experience with any addictive drug follows predictable progression. First, you might drink one glass of wine, and then you want another. Finally, you find yourself downing an entire bottle. As your drinking becomes heavier (and your addiction deeper), one glass is never enough. When people are on an addiction progression, most of the time, they are unaware of it. I certainly did not know early on that I was developing an alcohol problem. When you're at one glass of wine a night, two seems reasonable, and when you're at two, three doesn't seem that bad. Then you rationalize: I only had one bottle and didn't open the second one. And so on. And when I looked around, everyone I knew was in the same boat. In fact, I could easily see there were people worse off than I was. I had no idea I was the fly about to get eaten in the Venus flytrap. I was oblivious to the risk and to who I was becoming.

I also began to realize I was comparing myself to others instead of to my better or best self. This comparison trap of what constitutes an alcoholic—or not—is slippery. You're likely to be an alcoholic if you get a DWI. You're likely to be an alcoholic if you lose your job due to drinking. That said, what if you just had a bad night where you blacked out or a stressful period where you relied on heavy drinking to "get by"? Does this make you an alcoholic, or can XYZ circumstance account for your behavior, making the problem temporary and therefore not a real problem?

The questions I should have asked myself were these: Am I being a version of myself that I respect? Do I feel good about myself? Can I look at myself in the mirror at the end of the day? My answers to all those questions were an unequivocal NO. There is no medical definition for an alcoholic, so it is no surprise that many people who drink a lot may not identify with that label. By reminding myself that I was not the proverbial guy living under the bridge clutching his paper bag filled with a vodka bottle, I actually prevented myself from getting better, moving toward a better version of myself, and becoming a healthy version of myself.

Here's another thing about moderation. After a while, it became extremely difficult. I remember every day writing my goal that I would only have one glass (or at most two glasses) of wine a day, because that seemed "normal." Keep in mind that the CDC recommends that women drink no more than seven drinks in a week, which for a glass of wine means five fluid ounces—the sippy cup version of what many restaurants serve. I had thought that attempting moderation through a formal program like Moderation Management would give me the laser focus and discipline I needed to succeed. My functional self that had trained my body for half-marathon distance running and my mind for getting my MBA understood, even craved, rigor and rules. Still, I was failing. Cutting back was just so ... painful. When I look at my diary entries and notes in my calendar, I see it was my sole focus. I had to remember to be highly disciplined in social situations, and plan my drinking carefully, especially in business environments.

Eventually, this planning was entirely ruining my drinking experience, and I found myself deeply unhappy. If I could not drink how I wanted to and enjoy alcohol, what was the point? I was no longer having fun, and something needed to change. Would giving up alcohol entirely be easier than trying to stop after one or two drinks? Counterintuitively, the answer turned out to be yes.

Another important nugget that I discovered in my respect for moderation is the concept of a "hedonic set point." The hypothesis relating to addiction is that consistently high alcohol use over time sets a new dopamine point at which euphoria is achieved. If you've been drinking heavily and cut down, you never actually reach any type of relief because you never reach your set "happy" point, and your body keeps seeking out the missing dopamine. For me, drinking just a little felt like watching a party from outside through a glass window: I could observe, but I never actually participated in the event. My one or two drinks would leave me feeling unfulfilled and irritated. Eventually, when you stop drinking, happiness about things like hummingbirds, sunsets, and puppy dogs returns and you can get back to enjoying things that are normal.

What do you feel like after you have one or two drinks? Do you want more? Can you stop after one drink? Does it irritate you to have fewer drinks? Have you tracked your drinks HONESTLY over a period of a few weeks and analyzed how well you kept to a goal? Have you gone to an event without drinking and surprisingly had more fun because you were present and not thinking about drinking? Does moderation feel attainable to you?

Functional Part II: Advice and Helpful Tips

I am not a therapist, peer recovery specialist, doctor or scientist. I do not have a PhD in addiction studies. That said, my previous chapters established me as a person with functional alcohol use disorder. I definitely had a problem, but I have figured out how to maintain over six consecutive years of sobriety. I also have been successful in my career: I currently manage a department of seventy-one investment professionals as a director of operations. I have an MBA and several securities licenses. That said, my most important qualifier is this: I have figured out how to be free and I rarely think about alcohol. This combination of experiences and knowledge endows me with a special skill set to help you overcome your alcohol problem. I found out that some of the same skills that helped me be successful in the professional world may also be applicable to freeing yourself from alcohol.

Develop a Plan

Let's say that you have read up to this point and you are ready to give some of these ideas a shot. You are sick of hangovers. You are worried about going further down the black hole and anxious that you will not get out. Your significant other is tired of your shit. You replay the look your kid has on their face when they realize you are drunk. You may be functional, but you know your life is dysfunctional. You have finally hit the wall.

Well, let's do this! The next step is to make a plan. When you make a plan, you create a pathway to success, and as a Functional, you know what success looks like. A plan will give your brain a way to move forward and progress.

Keep in mind: Alcohol is an addictive drug, and it is everywhere. You are not going to magically conquer this thing without a plan, so I want you to take this next section seriously and commit to at least two ideas or more in the coming pages to try.

I want you to write down those two ideas after reading these sections. You can use the notes app on your phone or a piece of paper. You can

Functional

tack a note to your fridge. You can put a sticky on your bathroom mirror as a reminder. However you do it, put your intention in words out to the world. You are doing SOMETHING, and the universe needs to hear it.

Different people gravitate toward different solutions and recommendations. I want you to have an open mind and use whatever information works best for you. The following chapters are guidance toward freedom from alcohol. Some will resonate, some will not. There is a phrase in recovery that is relevant here: **Take what you want and leave the rest**.

Do not worry about failing. When we learn to ride a bike, a natural part of the process is usually falling. You may not fall, but you will not ride the bike without taking a risk. If you are reading this book, you are likely a Functional. You have been successful in your life, and you have had to work and achieve, and I am giving you a familiar path to follow as you work to become alcohol-free.

So, take out a pen. Or type the note in your app. Get ready. And MAKE A PLAN.

Commit to 30 Days of Not Drinking

I didn't start by saying I'd give up alcohol for good. I started by committing to a Sober September, which is a great way to baby-step yourself into a larger commitment. If you like to drink and are a daily drinker as I was, it probably feels completely crazy to say, "I will now stop drinking for the rest of my life." For my first sixty days of abstinence, I never thought of myself as "sober," because I fully believed I would go back to drinking.

A few weeks before I stopped drinking, I was reading a book by Rachel Hollis called *Girl, Wash Your Face*. I bought it because I liked the author's style and, in the book, she talks about problem drinking. I figured that, as a "normal girl" like me, she would have insights into my problem. She has a chapter called "The lie: I need a drink." I read it eagerly and, to be honest, it was good but not exactly what I needed. Another chapter focused on giving up anything for thirty days and in it, Rachel gives up Diet Coke. Naively, I thought, "Yes! Rachel's Diet Coke addiction is completely the same as my wine habit. I will do the same thing. If I can do thirty days without wine, alcohol will have no power over me, and I will no longer have a problem." While this was on its face an insane and stupid idea in hindsight, because Diet Coke is not addictive like alcohol, my brain got on board with the fuzzy logic, and I stopped drinking a few days before my actual Sober September started.

Dry January, Sober September, and Sober October are all well-known times during the year when many people take a break from drinking. One late August day, I surprised myself and my colleagues by showing up at happy hour for which I had coordinated a full corporate bar telling people I was doing Sober September. While quitting begets a million questions, taking a break is not only socially acceptable but even seen as smart, and it's the perfect excuse if you are not ready to tell people that you are giving up drinking (which I wasn't even sure I was really doing). It turned out that an executive vice president attended this happy hour, which I organized for the celebration of a major partnership.

She was a highly powerful leader in our organization with around four hundred people reporting to her. She noticed I was not drinking, and I said, "I'm doing a Sober September." She told me that she had taken a month off from drinking and found it extremely helpful. She had, she said, observed that too many events involved excess drinking, and she even added "good for you" at the end of her sentence. Her reaction reassured me, as I was super nervous about being in public for the first time and not drinking. To hear this industry leader affirm my choice was so incredible, and I felt instantly relieved. Her admiration and validation of my personal monthly challenge kept me going.

To this day, I can't tell you why the sober month stuck with me. I am not even sure how I was able to get past Day 3. I can tell you that as an achiever, I am intensely goal-focused, and I made having a sober month my sole goal. My plan was to take the month to explore the concept of not drinking and read everything I could about my "problem" while staying sober. There were times within my first seven days when I thought, "Screw this! I just want to drink! This is a dumb goal. And, come on, am I really bad enough that I need to stop?" But one sober month seemed like something I should be able to do.

Like many Functionals, I am a purposeful and focused person. *I ran a marathon. I completed an MBA. I should be able to not f'ing drink for thirty days!* So, I just kept plugging along. Some nights, I would be crabby, crave a glass of chardonnay, and end up just putting myself to bed early. I can honestly tell you, though, getting sober and staying sober has been the toughest fight of my life thus far. I give everyone trying to stay sober a huge round of applause, accolades, and warrior status: this battle is not easy—but it is worth it!

Although giving up alcohol for thirty days was tough, it was never as tough as waking up with hangxiety, constantly feeling ashamed, wondering what I might have done that I didn't remember, and knowing that I'd failed again at moderation. It took thirty days of feeling uncomfortable, but after that hump, I began to feel SO good! Around Day 7, I finally had the best sleep I'd had in years. It was *delicious*. As a Functional, achieving a goal such as thirty days sober gives you a huge boost in confidence and sense of achievement as well. Before, I would look in the mirror when I was getting ready for work and see my yellow eyes, dark under-eye circles, and blotchy skin. Gradually, my dull eyes started to brighten, and my skin rashes disappeared. Drinking can make you bloated, and my face and stomach started becoming slimmer and more toned. I ended up losing sixteen pounds in the first ninety days I was sober! Between the lost weight and de-bloating, people kept telling me, "You look great!" and the woman who stared back at me in the mirror was once again someone I felt proud to be.

I cannot think of any better way for someone to start the journey to freedom from alcohol, because the first thirty days were so transformative for me. Get through that first month, and do not look back.

Functional

It is important to offer a warning. Some people may be extremely physically addicted to alcohol and need to medically detox. This depends on your level of alcohol consumption and corresponding dependency. Unlike other addictive substances, alcohol is the one drug where detoxing too rapidly and without medical assistance can cause severe harm, even death. I was drinking close to two bottles a day of wine at my peak, but I did not need to go to detox or rehab and so cannot offer personal advice on either. I have, however, had several friends in recovery who needed one or both, and I do not know a single person who regretted taking advantage of those programs, despite some shame often associated with them and the major financial expense involved. Detox or rehab may be the first, next step.

My actual sober date is August 27, 2018. You will note that my goal was a sober September, but I started a few days early. I did this because I had a history of never going more than three days without drinking, and—planner that I am—I thought I might need a "test run" of a few days to ensure success for the coming month. Despite my denial, on a certain level, I knew full well I was physically addicted to alcohol. I remember that within the first week I did have "night sweats" from withdrawal.

Just Do This One Thing

"*Start by doing what's necessary; then do what's possible; and suddenly you are doing the impossible.*" — Francis of Assisi

After thirty days, not drinking got easier. I kept going with this alcohol-free thing. And to me, it was unbelievable. I had not gone more than three days without drinking in YEARS, and here I was, a month in and still going strong. The amazing thing was, while I had worried that not drinking would make me feel worse (and it did at first), after not too long it was making me feel better! I started sleeping better. I had more energy. I still had cravings, but overall, I felt pretty damn great.

Although I had work pressures, workout goals, groceries to buy, animals to feed, and a marriage to repair, I focused just on just this one thing: stay sober and become alcohol-free.

Since I knew a good deal of my feeling better was due to my no longer poisoning myself with an addictive substance, I became intellectually curious about discovering myself—my new self—and learning everything about being alcohol-free.

Functional

I would listen to podcasts, check out an AA meeting, find an online recovery community, and meet other sober people. Also, after the first thirty days, I began to focus my time specifically on staying alcohol-free. This meant staying away from triggering situations, giving myself good pep talks, and focusing on getting a nonalcoholic drink when I had to be in a boozy environment. I started to want people's help, found a sponsor, and began to listen to sober people when they gave me advice.

Soon I grew excited at the possibility of achieving an even loftier goal: I would stay sober for one whole year! This became my new, obsessive goal.

Now here is the crazy part. All I did was focus on one thing. I did not increase my workout goals. I did not try to improve my work output. I did not go on a diet or become vegan. My marriage was mostly good, but I did not try to improve my relationship.

And yet ... over the year of staying sober, with a focus solely on remaining alcohol-free, I quickly experienced massive and unequivocal positive changes in other parts of my life ... without even trying.

Here are some of the highlights:

- In about three months, I effortlessly lost sixteen pounds that had stubbornly clung to me for years. A medium glass of wine has 130 calories, which is as much as a chocolate donut. Before getting sober, I was easily "drinking" four donuts or more a night! When I stopped drinking, my calorie consumption became more normal. Also, liquor alters your taste buds, and when you quit drinking, your sense of smell and taste gets stronger. My food began to taste like three-star Michelin restaurant meals. I have always been a foodie, but I found myself purchasing higher quality ingredients and using more herbs in my meals, such as thyme or basil, because food tasted so good and I could actually discern food quality better.

- I had a whole lot more disposable income. I had been buying at least ten to twelve bottles of wine a week, taking Ubers to avoid driving under the influence, and spending too much money when I went out to restaurants and bars. I was easily blowing a grand a month in 2018 (before inflation) on drinking. That financial bleeding stopped when I went alcohol-free. Now, I spend more money on travel, saffiano leather handbags, higher quality clothes, and much less expensive mocktails. My restaurant tab has been drastically reduced.

- In the year I went alcohol-free, I was, surprisingly, promoted at work from senior product manager to director. I had always been a hard worker, but my boss now told me, "I have to promote you, because you're too good for another leader not to poach." He even purchased an ice cream cake for my team for celebration. In the year I became sober, I became totally focused on my work (naturally, without conscious effort) and had endless energy after a great night's sleep.

- My marriage improved. The first few months, my husband did not really know what to think about my being sober. Would I go back or stay this way? That said, he was impressed with how many days I had gone without having a drink. I also was spending a lot of time learning about how to stay sober. He could see that I was trying and succeeding, and he celebrated all my milestones with me including my one-year mark. He was supportive and has told me many times that he "likes sober Rachel."

- My sleep improved tremendously. Alcohol impacts your rapid eye movement (REM) sleep, which is your deepest sleep cycle. Scientists do not know exactly why REM sleep is so important, but studies show that even a single drink will negatively affect your sleep quality. After I stopped drinking, I finally felt well rested and popped out of bed every morning with a smile on my face. Sober sleep is still one of my favorite benefits of going alcohol-free.

Functional

- No joke, I began to manifest things that I have always wanted. My home became more beautiful because I had more energy to keep it clean, and things that had always bothered me in certain rooms now became intolerable and I moved to have them fixed. I also began to connect with people at work I admired but had previously avoided because they'd seemed too intimidating. The things, people, and environments I desired now came to me, simply because I was actually present to receive them. In addition, I rejected things and behaviors that were no longer meeting my new, higher standards. I couldn't spend time with people who gossiped or complained all day, because their actions did not match my vibe.

I have met people who try to complete too many changes all at once. They try to go alcohol-free, work out at the gym daily, find a new mate, etc., and they do not always become successful because they've taken on too many goals all at once. If you're looking to get sober, I strongly recommend just doing this one thing for a year. After the year, you will have survived all the holidays and weddings sober and stopped old habits, and you will wake up a year later realizing that your life is completely different. JUST DO THIS ONE THING!

Get It Out of Your House

"If you don't want to slip up, don't go where it is slippery." — Alcoholics Anonymous

If you really want to give this a shot, you need THE wine, THE beer, THE whiskey, THE whatever OUT of the house. Get IT out.

It does not matter if you have spent $200 to $10,000 on alcohol that's sitting in your home. It must go. Yes, you can put it in the garbage. You can give it away. You can have it held somewhere or sell it if you have an expensive, multi-thousand-dollar wine cellar. You just need it outside of your house where you can't get to it.

Your home is your sanctuary. It is where you eat, where you rest, and where you may have your family or pets. Right now, your brain is thinking that alcohol *is* your home, and it needs to be reprogrammed to understand that alcohol is *not* home.

I personally threw away about $300 worth of wine. I asked my husband to help me. I did it because he is a rule keeper and if I bought more, I knew he would say, "Rachel, we just threw away your wine and you don't need more."

Functional

What if you live in a house where other people drink, and they want to keep alcohol? I would suggest that you ask them to keep it someplace else. A woman I know told her husband that there would be no alcohol in their immediate house. If he wanted to drink, he had to keep his alcohol in the garage. He put his beer in a mini-fridge in his garage and would go out there if he wanted to drink. By moving the alcohol outside the house, she felt like she could control her environment and her access to alcohol, which helped her stay sober, and this worked for the couple because they were both respecting each other's boundaries.

If someone in your house is upset by your boundaries, you can tell them that this is what you need right now. If they love you or are your friend, it should not be that hard for them to keep alcohol out of your living quarters. You're not asking them to stop drinking. But you are asking them to support your effort to get sober. You may eventually be fine with having it in the house in the future when you are stronger, but in the beginning, it needs to go.

I no longer have any alcohol in my home. Its presence disturbs my mental peace, and I consider it a crap substance. I have a rule that if we entertain and people want to bring it over, they can. But they must also take it home with them when they leave. My muscle memory is too strong. If I see a half-drunk bottle of wine, I do not want my brain to be consumed thinking the bottle needs to be drunk.

Get it out. Get it out! You are much more likely to be successful without alcohol in your home.

If you do not drink at home, but you visit a neighborhood bar or restaurant where you drink, you need to remove yourself from that place. It could be temporary, or it could be forever, but you need not worry about that right now. You just need to give yourself and your plan a chance to be successful. This means you need to break your pattern of stopping by the place where you drink. If this means driving the long way home from work to avoid going on autopilot and ending up in the parking lot of the liquor store, so be it.

Do I believe you can be successful staying sober while staring at a chilled bottle of chardonnay every time you open your fridge door? Honestly, no. I was over two years sober and my brother-in-law moved in with us for a while. He put a case of beer in our fridge, and I just became irritated and discontented when I saw it. I didn't even like beer, but it was messing with my brain. I finally asked my husband to talk to him. It was a "me" issue, but I just needed it out of my home. I am sure someone could be successful, but I want to give you the highest probability of success. Our brains have been trained hundreds, thousands, even millions of times to pick up that bottle and pour a glass ... or more. Like Pavlov's dog, my mouth would salivate the moment I opened the fridge door and saw the bottle waiting for me, available and ready to pour.

Give your poor mind fewer things to focus on and get alcohol out of your home. You can thank me later.

Tapering and Detox

I am not an expert on this next topic, tapering, but exactly how you decrease your alcohol consumption is an important safety consideration. Tapering, which is recommended, especially if you drink heavily, is the process of gradually reducing the amount of alcohol you consume to avoid withdrawal symptoms. If you are drinking a lot, you are likely to have a chemical dependency on alcohol. Some withdrawal symptoms include anxiety, tremors, sweating, nausea, vomiting, headaches, and delirium tremens (DTs). If you have ever experienced these when you have temporarily stopped drinking or not had access to alcohol, you likely need to taper or undergo medical detox.

I will share that I was drinking between one and two bottles of wine a night, every night, with the body of a forty-something female who weighed about 140 pounds. I did not taper and went cold turkey. On the third day of my sobriety, I did have night sweats, a low-grade headache, and an upset stomach. These symptoms were not terrible, but they were not great. They seemed to last about twenty-four hours. This was my process, so be sure to consider the safest approach that will work best for you. If you are not drinking excessively and think you can go cold turkey, you might try it, especially if you keep failing at moderation. But if you start to experience serious withdrawal symptoms, you may need to go to a hospital or detox facility.

It may not be feasible for you to immediately quit drinking. I asked you to write down two items from these chapters you will try to be successful, and if your plan is to taper first, that is an acceptable plan. Tapering is a harm reduction approach, and you are moving yourself in the right direction. Better is better.

Here are some safe ways you can taper:

- **Gradual reduction of your drink of choice.** If you are drinking six glasses of wine a night, you can try reducing to five glasses a night for the next three or four nights. After that, you may be able to move to four glasses for the next three or four nights, then three, and so on. Once you are at two glasses a night, see if you can go to zero.

- **Dilute your drinks.** If you drink wine, you can have wine spritzers instead of a full glass of wine. If you are drinking five glasses of wine, try five spritzers. Either that or try drinking a glass of water or sparkling water for every alcoholic drink you have. This method can be tricky, because you need to ensure that you are properly measuring and not overcompensating.

- **Switch up your drink of choice for an alternative with less alcohol.** Many articles online actually recommend tapering with beer. If you do not drink beer, this may be helpful because it immediately gets you away from your drink of choice and may help you be successful. I have always hated beer since it makes you belch and tastes hoppy, so if you're like me, switching to beer might help you cut back quickly on your drinking.

Functional

With all the taper recommendations, I would get out a calendar and plan on what days you'll transition down. Moderation can be pure hell, and using the calendar is a control method to decrease your drinking. You may notice you are in a bad mood for a month. By limiting your alcohol consumption, you are also decreasing your sugar intake, so you can add some chocolate or sweets to help lessen the symptoms of sugar withdrawal.

NOTE: Alcohol withdrawal can be fatal and may require supervision. In fact, alcohol, benzos, and opioids are some of the drugs for which detox is typically covered by insurance, so please consider professional, medical help if you need it. If you are a Functional, you may consider it the most humiliating thing in the world to put yourself in a detox program. As a Functional, we do not like to admit weakness, and we are more comfortable being stoic, striving to improve, and being an example to others. That said, detox may be just the thing that sets you up for success safely, especially if you are frequently drinking a high level of alcohol.

Making Friends in Sobriety and Sober Communities

When I first began to realize I was going to stay sober, I knew I needed to find more sober friends and people with other interests than drinking. There is a saying that you are a reflection of the five people you spend time with. Well, the five people I spent the most time with were all winos. "The winos" was the nickname I had for the friends I consistently hung out with. No surprise then that I drank with them.

I put a lot of effort into making friends, and I know keeping friendships and making new ones is a primary concern for people getting sober. Therefore, I created an exhaustive list to help you. I will tell you what I did but also provide you with other options to consider.

My social skills are decent. I live with a husband who has social anxiety and finds large crowds and meeting strangers challenging, so I am the more social one in our marriage. My approach may be too outgoing for you if you are shy or uncomfortable meeting new people, but I do feel this list will be helpful to you.

Functional

Also, all my friends and family (except my husband) drank, so joining sober communities felt out of my comfort zone. But once I started meeting people in recovery, I found them to be a lot like me, and we shared many similar experiences.

Join a Group

I went to an AA meeting on Day 14, and as many of you will experience, people there are always happy to give you a number or a phone list. Use it or friend someone in a meeting on social media. In many cases, these friendships will develop organically. I met a woman in my home group who loved Orangetheory Fitness. I had never tried it, so we went to a few classes together, which was fun. I got a chance to get to know her better and get into a great, upbeat workout. In my AA meetings, I met women who asked me out for coffee, invited me to dream board sessions, movie nights, and rigorous hikes. You would be surprised how many Functionals there are in AA meetings! I have been to meetings with lawyers, doctors, and recognizable TV figures. I will discuss AA in more detail, but it can be a surprisingly easy place to meet people.

I also joined Recovery Elevator (RE), an online recovery group. Recovery Elevator is a podcast that also has a Facebook group to which you can subscribe. The cost is $24 a month, but the value totally outweighed the cost for me—and was a small fraction of what I'd been spending on alcohol. They have four different groups capped at 350 people, and a group with people from all over the world but mostly the US. I attended

Functional

some of their virtual meetups and met others in person in my state. When I traveled out of state, I made a point of meeting up with other members and felt happy and connected and found it easier to stay sober while traveling. RE had a sixty-plus person meetup in Minneapolis where I met great, local people in recovery, and this led me to form a private Facebook group for my local RE people. For our first in-person get-together we held a dry event at a local bar that featured mocktails and we had a blast! I went to meetups in Nashville and Atlanta. I met up with another member in Miami. I also had coffee with another woman visiting Minnesota from Oregon. RE really was an effortless way to connect.

There are now even more wonderful online sober communities, especially since the pandemic. A great online community is the We Are the Luckiest Sobriety Support group. Many people are sober-curious or new in their sobriety journey. They have several meetings that members can participate in on any given day from an app on your phone. Members can listen in their cars or as they drive to work or in their homes late at night, and there is no requirement for cameras to be on to participate in a meeting. Online groups are great for Functionals, especially at first, because of the fear of seeing someone you know—or who knows you—at an in-person AA meeting (although AA now has more online meetings). Struggles with alcohol are deeply personal, and it is helpful being in a community of people that is easily—and often anonymously—accessible online.

Follow: Social Media

There is a wonderful sober Instagram and TikTok community. You can find sober influencers by following sober hashtags like #sober #alcoholfree #wearetheluckiest. I soon found people in my state who were publicly sober. Some sober groups, such as Sober Girls Society, also put up "Find your sober tribe" posts, on which people will post their city and state, and you can comment if you live close by and want to meet. Sober influencers show their lifestyle in a positive, upbeat light, which helps you feel motivated, especially during the early days of your sobriety journey.

I also listened to recovery podcasts and joined their secret Facebook groups. I listened to *Unruffled*, a podcast about art and women in sobriety, and once inside their group, saw they had a members list with people's locations listed. There was a member right in my city. From Facebook, I could tell she looked about my age and had a husband and kids. I sent her a message and we met up for coffee, then for walks, and then traveled together for a recovery event.

Another tip I would recommend for social media is to hide all alcohol ads from your feeds. Once you do this, the platform's algorithm will

Functional

no longer show these to you. In addition, if your friend Becky is always posting pretty glasses or wine or boat sunsets with beer, it may be healthy for you to mute her temporarily. You want to be successful. You can always go back to seeing Becky's posts when you are stronger and alcohol holds no appeal (trust me, it can happen). Google how to hide alcohol ads on your social media feeds—this will really change your trajectory.

Lead and Step Out

Find people with a common interest that's distinct from staying sober. Have you always wanted to be an early morning hiker, but you were previously too hungover for that version of yourself? Do you like pickleball or arts and crafts? Focus on meeting people who share interest in a primary activity that does not involve drinking. For me, I had always wanted to go on a yoga retreat, but I was thinking I needed a heavy amount of wine, and I was too unhealthy to participate. I have now completed three yoga retreats in Mexico, Texas, and Costa Rica, where I wake up and practice yoga early in the morning—without a hangover. The retreat in Costa Rica I trained for, because we did about three to four hours of yoga a day! I remember being in the yoga shala with mats and blocks, surrounded by other yogis in warrior I pose staring at the Costa Rican jungle, and hearing howler monkeys. I found it both unbelievable that I was in this place, while I also knew it was exactly where I was meant to be.

I even organized my own damn get-togethers. Early on, I just wanted to meet women in a non-AA setting. I wanted to have fun without the booze! I organized a coffee meetup with another sober woman at a

Functional

local coffee shop with a private room that I was able to rent for free. At first there were only four of us, but shortly after, more women started coming. Another woman in the group started organizing events as well, and we had lunch with six other women at a new cosmopolitan restaurant with a beautiful atrium that served delicious mocktails. You can formally start a meetup group on meetup.com for an interest or coordinate a few women you know for a group meeting. Pre-COVID, I hosted a few sober women meetups at a coffee shop that would allow larger groups to secure group rooms if guests purchased food and drinks from their restaurant. Because it was a larger, but close space, people felt comfortable sharing, and I made great friends that way.

At the end of the book, I list recommended resources. Take a second to scan and search online for those options. Hopefully, one will make your plan.

Deal With Your REAL Problem

Some people will never stay sober if they do not deal with the real reason that they drank in the first place. This could be a big "T" trauma like rape, incest, or racial injustice. It could be a little "t" trauma like a coworker who consistently excludes you from plans. You could be working with abuse or neglect from your significant other. You could have a child with special needs, a parent who is dying, or a cross-addiction such as an eating disorder or smoking weed.

I do not know what your REAL problem may be. I do know that if you constantly numb yourself with a substance like alcohol, you never actually fix a problem. It keeps you stuck in the same bad job, bad relationship, or bad situation that you may have used as an excuse to numb yourself.

I would "drink at" the same situations repeatedly instead of dealing with them constructively. Here is an example. I used to have work stress that I thought was unavoidable, often in the form of difficult people I had to work with and put up with their behavior, because that is what I was paid to do. It frustrated me that I could not do anything about it (or so I thought), so I would drink at it instead. This made me feel better—until the next morning when I was hungover with a splitting headache. At some point, I began working with a therapist who helped me with stress techniques, but a breakthrough for me was finding a work coach who listened to my issues at work and constructively helped me solve them. I received tips and tricks, and she coached me through situations I felt inadequate to handle. I completed two thirty-minute sessions with her a month for a minimal fee, and that was some of the best money I have ever spent.

I remember there was a scenario I worked on where a manager below me yelled at me first, said something was my fault, then cried in an hour-long meeting. I had never had anyone who worked for me conduct themselves in such an aggressive and passive-aggressive way. I told my coach I had to go to work each day but came home and was in bed by 6 p.m. because I was so exhausted from the exchange and having to deal with HR meetings. She told me this was new territory for me, and it was not surprising that my body wanted extra rest, and she gave me permission to just allow it to happen. Instantly, I felt validated and reasonable, and I could move through the challenge more comfortably.

In many cases, it may be a good idea to get a therapist and work through your issues. Be honest about your drinking as well so your therapist can help you.

Many people have another REAL problem or underlying issue. And a handful of people I know came to understand that they did not have childhood trauma or a "bad life" yet just kept consuming an addictive substance.

Write a Breakup Letter to Your Substance

When you are first getting sober, your mind may be all over the place. On the one hand, what I am telling you sounds great: As a Functional, you will want to conquer this issue, become your best self, and you may already be rehearsing your one-year sobriety speech in the mirror. On the other hand, there is the little devil perched on your shoulder telling you that a drink will make everything better and maybe you really do not have a problem because you have not lost your job or spouse or gotten a DWI ... yet.

Try this: I want you to write a breakup letter to your drug of choice. I have read this breakup letter when I was in the ladies' room at a restaurant that was serving wine flights that looked intoxicating, and I have read it parked outside a bike store that I had driven to that turned out to be next to the largest Total Wine in my state. Sitting in that parking lot, I honestly wondered if I was going to buy the hybrid Trek I'd gone to find or three bottles of my favorite chardonnay on sale. I read my breakup letter that I had stored on my phone and just drove out of that lot because I knew I did not want to start drinking, go back

Functional

to being abused by wine, and stop being the best version of myself that I had become.

Here are some tips for writing the letter:

- I recommend you take a solid twenty minutes and write a breakup letter to your drink of choice.

- I want you to put this letter in your phone somewhere and/or keep a physical letter near you—inside your purse or glove box. It needs to be close to you, and you have easy access to read it at a critical point in time. For me, I have it in the notes app on my phone; I can search "breakup" or "letter," and it comes up easily in the search results.

- Think of the key moments and situations where it absolutely felt like you were being used by the substance you are breaking up with. Who have you hurt? How have you hurt yourself? How did you feel powerless and "unfunctional"?

- A favorite recommendation of mine is to write what it feels like to be hungover. Have you been so hungover that it lasted longer than twenty-four hours or you missed a key meeting or activity you needed or wanted to attend? Did you have a pounding headache or spend the night vomiting?

- Make your letter powerful and raw. For example, one friend of mine wrote about how many times they'd shit themselves in the back of an Uber and repeatedly woke up with their bedsheets full of piss. Your letter is supposed to be real. Its purpose is to remind you of your experience with alcohol: if you are in an environment that is triggering, turning to the letter will help shift your mind to the truth so you can avoid a relapse.

Write a Breakup Letter to Your Substance

Here is my unedited breakup letter with wine:

Dear wine,

I used to think that you brought me friends, coping skills, and helped me achieve greatness at work. I now know this was a lie.

It was not fun when I drank so much and tried to take out my contacts and could not. I woke up the next morning with a terribly red eye and had to go to an eye doctor. After the eye doctor kindly removed pieces of contacts from my eye that I managed to rip, with concern she told me that I could have severely damaged my eye. "Why didn't you come in, honey, instead of hurting your eye so bad?!" That was a blast, and I had a terrible-looking eye for a week and felt like a deranged maniac wasting a kind doctor's time dealing with my drunk consequence.

It was such a joy when your soulmate husband who built you a home and always tells you that you are gorgeous asked you with tears in his eyes "Rachel, why am I not enough? Why do you need wine?" This conversation was especially terrible because you knew he grew up with an alcoholic mother and his childhood was so hard. Yeah, that was fun.

How about all the times that you told yourself that you would cut down or reduce your wine and you could not? Remember all the times that you woke up with shame and a hangover? All those conversations really made you hate yourself and provided you with low self-confidence. Oh, this was winning!

Wine, you were a huge liar. You tried to break up a marriage and you made me doubt my abilities. You are a drug just like crack, cocaine, and cigarettes and I am done being owned by you. Alcohol, you are shit.

No kind regards,

Rachel

Date Yourself: #Selfcare That Is Real

Many people agree that part of addiction is not loving yourself and not taking care of your deeper needs. The modern-day women's Instagram is filled with hashtags about self-care that feature women drinking wine. How can drinking a toxin be considered #selfcare?

One concept I embraced early in sobriety is the idea of dating yourself. I used to ask myself, "What would Rachel want"? Before I became sober, Rachel mostly wanted wine. I even have a social media post about getting the laundry done on a Sunday and going out to a winery with friends. Now, I view self-care as something that hits a pit of a need, and I can tell you that I feel more fulfilled with healthy versions of self-care than a glass—or bottle—of poison that made me feel like crap in the morning.

Do you remember when you were first dating someone, and you were so interested in that person that you wanted to know everything about them. What was their favorite food? What activity did they like to do? Did they read autobiographies or fiction? What was their favorite animal? Do they like vacations on the beach or in the mountains? Ask yourself questions about yourself. What do you actually like beyond drinking?

A great form of self-care is to date yourself. Ask yourself: If I had a free afternoon and no constraints, what would I like to do? Would I like to go out and explore a cute little shop? Would I like a manicure or pedicure? Would I like to be in a luxurious, but comfortable sweater? Would I like to read a book or watch something on Netflix? A funny thing I notice is that when it is just me asking myself what I want to do, I assert that I want a particular food that my partner does not like to eat. For example, my husband likes to eat red meat, and when we go out, it may be to a burger place, which is fine for a "couple" date. But if I get to choose for myself, it may be soup or some type of ethnic food he would not enjoy. Another form of self-care I love is Epsom salt baths. I have regretted drinking wine, but I have never regretted having a bath. A great bath before you go to sleep feels calming and helps me sleep.

I also really enjoy reading. I love to go into a bookstore and pick through some items to read. I will walk through the aisles, browsing titles and carefully choosing my book. I will pick up many books, read their descriptions, and walk from shelf to shelf. I will then go to the magazine section and soak up the visual covers. I typically land on a home or design magazine. Maybe it is spring, and the cover tells you how to create a beautiful porch or patio with visions of relaxation and sumptuous patterns. I dug that shit up. I will go and pay for the book and then head to the coffee shop for tea and read my finds with utter abandonment as I people-watch.

Sometimes dating yourself can take on additional luxury. I know women who like to purchase lingerie for themselves only and not their partner or buy themselves beautiful jewelry. For one of my soberversaries, I purchased a $150 luxury friendship bracelet with beautiful gold plates and an engraving of a phrase that I love with my sober date. It is an expensive friendship bracelet, but it is beautiful and even sits in a lovely case in my jewelry drawer. I feel beautiful and safe whenever I wear

Functional

it. It has a gold accent, and I find myself matching my outfits to that bracelet, because I love how I feel when I wear it.

Sometimes, I just need a nap and sleep feels luxurious. I will work Monday through Friday and on Saturday afternoon, I will take a forty-five-minute nap. I have cozy, warm blankets, and the shades will be drawn. There will be no phones in my bedroom and only a fan for white noise. I will sleep deeply. I will wake up and feel refreshed and invincible.

Another thing I love to do is get my hair done. I love the smell of Aveda products, and I will go to a nicer salon to get a haircut. They wash your hair and give you a scalp massage. The products smell wonderful and are not harmful to your hair. The stylist gives you a smart cut that just makes you feel better about how you look and cuts out the weight of your hair and dead, lifeless locks. She also gives you a blowout, which can be worn the following day without much effort. All you have to do is sit in a chair and read a magazine or stare at your phone. It is lovely and relaxing.

"Who Am I Exercises?"

When you begin to get sober and stop drinking, you suddenly realize you are no longer a zombie, and you start to wake up. It is as if you arise from the matrix. You look around and you are like, "You know what? I really hate parties where everyone is loud and drunk," or "I remember this childhood activity I used to do and why did I stop doing it?" I found this exercise in a writing class I took. (Thank you, Ann Dowsett Johnston, for introducing me to this concept.) Alcohol numbs emotions and personality. As we stop drinking, we begin to ask ourselves, "Who am I?" To help you begin to define yourself, try writing out "I am" or "I am not" statements. These do not have to be literal, but they should feel authentic and true. They also do not always have to be serious. Silliness is encouraged. Here are some examples:

- I can spend hours looking at little shops filled with books, home furnishings, clothing, or artist findings.

- I am not a person who can stand long periods at a Monster Truck rally.

- I am a person who believes that nuts ruin a dessert. I mean, do you ever get excited over a cupcake sprinkled with peanuts?

Functional

- I am a worrier. It is a natural state, and it is what I primarily go to therapy these days for.

- I find writers to be the true artists of our time.

- My favorite month of the year is September. The weather is perfect: sunny, but a little breezy and the trees are in full fall foliage.

- After the rights that we lost when Roe v. Wade was overturned, I became a single ticket voter.

- Growing up, it never even occurred to me that I would be a fixed income trader and a director in investments; instead, I thought I would be an English literature teacher.

- I wish I could speak better Spanish.

- I am an Enneagram Type 1 (Perfectionist).

- I sometimes talk about writers as if they are people I truly know in real life.

- I am not a person who can live without coffee.

- Words have meaning, so I am conscious about how I explain that I am not drinking. I say that I am alcohol-free. That said, I will identify as an alcoholic when I am in an AA room, because I am in a safe place with peers who will not judge that word.

- In my six years of recovery, I have been to hundreds of AA meetings, and I can honestly say I have not been to a bad one.

- Animal causes deserve extra financial commitment. Animals have no money and cannot advocate for themselves, unlike people.

- Science was my worst subject in school, and it honestly bores me.

- I could decorate my home for hours and I should have been an interior designer.

- I cannot stand clutter, disorganization, environments that are abandoned and an utter mess.

- Flowers and plants make me happy, and I can spend hours at gardening stores.

- I am really good with money, although it is something I don't always like to admit around women. In my forty-eight years, I really have not let anyone manage my money but myself and it teaches you that there are a lot of expensive investments and brokers who care more about their retirement accounts than your retirement accounts.

Tips for Going Out

It is not surprising that many people can be uncomfortable socially and reach for a drink to relax around people. Especially if you are a full-grown adult, you have been trained to believe that socializing *requires* a drink in your hand. You may have come from a background where your whole family drank or attended a college where drinking games and keg parties were a big part of the experience. Your work environment may be "a little boozy," which is how one of my employers described a department's culture when I asked them to tell me about the team.

Going out without drinking is likely to be new to you, and I want you to put yourself in the best framework possible. Going back to the purpose of Part II of the book, this may be the chapter you need to set yourself up for success. Functionals are often in powerful positions, such as managers or influencers of people, because we can lead and perform. You may work in sales or must regularly attend social gatherings to nurture your career. Even if you are not a people person, you may have to navigate a wedding or get-together where there will be drinking—and that may be triggering.

Tips for Going Out

Below are some helpful tips for a successful outcome at your next social event:

Tip #1: Your first goal when you walk through the door is to get a drink in your hand—an alcohol-free drink

Party hosts want to be good entertainers and will want to ensure that their guests are comfortable. If they ask, "Can I get you a drink?" you do not need to launch into a long explanation of why you are not drinking alcohol. Instead, simply say, "I'd like a soda, thanks," or sparkling water, or just water. Your hosts do not need to hear that you are not drinking because you have a problem, or even that you're going sober for a month. The host just wants to get you settled, so they can move on to the next person. In addition, getting a drink in your hands will also make you comfortable and you will blend in with the rest of the guests. Really, no one cares about what you are actually drinking or not drinking; it is good social practice to have a beverage in your hand. In addition, I will tell you that I have had people put glasses of wine in my hand out of habit, thinking of how the old Rachel used to operate and not aware I had become alcohol-free. These good-intentioned folks believed they were doing me a favor and thought they were cleverly anticipating my needs. Put a nonalcoholic drink in your hand right away, and this will never happen.

If you are going to a bar or restaurant, your goal is the same, but you are more likely to succeed as you can order your drink of choice. If I have a business dinner, I normally look up the menu online to review their nonalcoholic drink options. All places will have some type of nonalcoholic beverage. My bar drink is typically sparkling water or club soda with lime. There are also fun mocktails and shrubs, and most margaritas and mojitos can be made virgin or nonalcoholic.

Tip #2: Make sure you are not hungry, angry, lonely, or tired (HALT) when you walk into the room

If you are typically exhausted by 5 p.m. after working all day and you arrive at a bar at 7 p.m. yawning as you walk through the door, you may be too tired to make a good decision and not drink, especially in early sobriety. If you walk into a bar where drinking is what everyone comes to do, and while you are starving, they offer miniature plates of air food for "dinner," you may be much more likely to drink. If you're concerned you won't be able to get enough food, plan to eat beforehand. I always try to have a package of nuts in my purse—an easy snack with protein to fill me up.

If you are angry or lonely, it can be helpful to have friends you can text while in the bathroom or on the way to the event. These can be other sober friends or your spouse or someone close to you who is supporting the success of your sobriety goal. Having a wingman or wing woman as you navigate a boozy room can be a godsend. If it just gets to be too much, head to the bathroom, text your person, and tell them, "I saw the wine flights and walked right by" or "I'm taking a break in the loo from all the damn drunk people." It will make you feel less angry and lonely to have a friend.

In addition, it can be great to tell one person you know and trust you are trying to be sober/alcohol-free. I had a coworker who had been sober for a long time, and I told them I was not drinking when I was around nine months sober. They stuck around me for the happy hour we both had to attend and made sure we had ample alcohol-free drinks. I have also had people attend events who knew I was not drinking regardless of whether they were or not. If they were good friends and good people, I would end up talking to them after the crowd was too intoxicated.

As a worst-case scenario, just bail out on the whole event. If you think your odds are low for sticking to your plan, just do not attend. You can say you are sick, have another obligation, or something came up. Keep to your plan, and if you worry attending an event will be too much, do not go. Remember, this is a temporary situation. As you grow stronger by being alcohol-free, you will not feel like you are walking on newfound baby deer legs.

Tip #3: Practice the art of the "no goodbye" and leave when you need to

I am from the Midwest, and when we leave any event, a long goodbye ensues. You need to hug and kiss aunts, uncles, cousins, in-laws, moms, and dads, and make plans to see people again. When we leave a happy hour, we thank the hosts or the senior management who threw the event. It is polite and good manners. That said, no one is checking a list to make sure you say your goodbyes, and you will not be faulted for simply leaving. There have been times when I have just been DONE with an event and ducked out. No one cried—or died—because I left early.

In general, after people have a couple of drinks, they enter a different world. They are more relaxed and may even begin repeating themselves. You can feel like you are not even conversing with a real person. An easy excuse is to say you need to use the restroom, head there, then walk out of the event when you are done. You also can duck out of a conversation by politely excusing yourself to talk to someone else with the phrase, "It was lovely to chat with you. I see so and so over there, and I need to tell them about such and such. I'll catch up with you later."

It may also be helpful to think of an excuse before the event. For example, if you know you are probably going to leave the party early, let people at the event know you can only stay for a short time, or even inform the host prior before the event that you have a time constraint. For example, you could tell the host you are coming for the first couple of hours but need to leave early because you promised to pick someone up at 7 p.m. This gives you a good excuse not to drink and a reasonable explanation

Functional

for leaving, and it presents you as being polite. You could also say you have a long drive ahead or must get up early. If it is a brunch or midday event, you can say you have to be home to prepare dinner or get ready for the next day.

The end of the night can be a perfect time to escape the obligation, walk out the door with your head held high that you made it through the event without drinking, and strut confidently down the street to your car or Uber. Your pillow and cozy blankets may call you to bed, where you will sleep soundly, and you nod off without worrying about things you said or not remembering how you got home. When you wake up the next day, you will know that you kept your promise to yourself—and you won't have a hangover. True story: I have never met anyone who regretted NOT drinking the night before, but I have met many who ABSOLUTELY regretted drinking the night before.

Tip #4: Bring your own drinks

It would be impolite and rude to bring your own drinks into a restaurant, but it may be sensible if you are headed over to someone's home. I love sparkling water of any flavor but honestly hate most soft drinks like Coke or Mountain Dew. It is easier to bring your own, and many hosts will be relieved because you will be relaxed. Sometimes, hosts will not know your drink, or maybe they remember the "old" you who drank endless glasses of prosecco. Instead, control your outcome and bring your own drink to the backyard party or event. That way, you know exactly what you are going to drink.

Tip #5: Call your shot

If after you read all these tips and you still feel nervous, stop for a second. Think about how you managed going out in public previously. Perhaps you attended a party a year ago and started drinking from your entry through the door when the host handed you a drink and pointed out the bar for refills. Perhaps your boss is a heavy drinker and buys a round of shots for the team on a regular basis. You clearly have an idea of how the night could go, so start planning for how you can make it go differently.

In addition, if you have been in the same environment and you ended up drinking more than you wanted, remember how you felt the next day and what that looked like. Were you hungover? Did you have to apologize for something you said? Did you have to go back to get your car the next day because you were too drunk to drive home? Did you black out? Take note of what happened. With that in mind, call your shot and plan a better outcome. Would your chances of staying alcohol-free increase if you had a friend you could text if things got too intense? Line that friend up before the event and bring them in on your plan. Are you worried about going to a packed bar or someone handing you an alcoholic drink or placing one in front of you? You may need to research the venue's drink menu ahead of time or just bring your own beverage. When you "call your shot," you bring comfort to your mind, and you give it the tools to handle something with which it may be unfamiliar. Planning can not only provide a favorable outcome, but it also reduces anxiety.

Keep It Front and Center: Family Pictures, Affirmations, Talismans, and Tattoos

A while ago, I took an online course that was preparatory for me to pass an exam. At the very first class, the instructor did the usual kickoff and explained the syllabus and key milestones we would cover over the semester. It was a standard first class until the seasoned instructor did something unique: He asked us if we had a picture of our family or pet close by. The class was online, and I was sitting in my office at the time and staring at a picture of my husband and my black cat. He guided us to pick up the picture, look at it closely and think about why we were sacrificing our time for our family and pets. We were taking the exam to improve our stature in life and gain expertise in our profession to improve the lives of our family. He asked us to focus 100 percent of our time when we were with him as well as our study time on preparing for the exam so that we could pass it on the first try. He reminded us to look at our family to think about the home renovations, college expenses, retirements, and trips we would ultimately have if we focused our time deliberately on our studies. I have thought about this advice a lot when I am somewhere or doing something I am not excited about now. These physical reminders such as the picture that evoke emotion can serve to sharpen your focus on your life priorities.

My guess is that if you are a Functional, you are good at responsibility to a partner, wife, employer, husband, child, or pet. A Functional fundamentally knows how to love and care for beings that are important to them. If keeping a sobriety goal is new to you, think of that family picture or pet front and center as the reason why you are taking the next step. A good motivation can be keeping a family photo on your phone as a screensaver or a physical family photo in a room in your home where you have traditionally drunk before. This will keep you focused on your goal and remind you why you are doing a harder task now, such as not drinking, to keep the people and things that you love safe and happy in the future.

Affirmations

About a year after I went alcohol-free, I found a great happiness and productivity app that I still use daily: the Five-Minute Journal app. Everyone will tell you that gratitude lists, reflections on what you want to accomplish, and affirmations will change your life. This app is fast: It only takes five minutes. It also records your life, so you can go back, and you begin to see patterns. I have a few affirmations I write daily in this app that I recommend: "I thrive in my alcohol-free life" or "Trust sober magic."

When you write an affirmation statement daily, your mind becomes focused on your goal, and it also becomes comfortable with something that is unfamiliar. I like to type out my goal and say it aloud to reinforce what I want to occur. I use the statement "Trust sober magic" more often lately, and to me it means I just must stay sober for the day and that is the only goal for the day. When I trust sober magic, the universe provides me with a solution if I show up ready and of clear mind and body to receive that solution. Like the family photo exercise, you can also add it to your phone as a background or as a reminder in your calendar of what your goal is.

Talismans and Tattoos

In my first few months of being sober, I understood that this thing I was doing was delicate. I still had clear and vivid memories of waking up with a hangover, and I just wanted to keep the good life that I was now creating for myself. I had heard about someone buying themselves a piece of jewelry with their sobriety date engraved. I loved this idea, because I could think of bars and restaurants where I needed to be, and I thought it would be helpful to have a talisman I could look at and use as my secret support to maintain my goal that I wanted to keep in earnest.

I purchased a bracelet on Etsy based on an R. S. Grey quote that said, "She believed that she could, so she did." On the back of the bracelet was my sobriety date. The quote is empowering and speaks about overcoming a challenge. I did not want to go back to a feeling of disappointment and go against that version of myself who had accomplished this amazing thing. I remember having to sit through a work dinner at a steakhouse where I was the only person not drinking. I kept placing my fingers over my bracelet wrist, over the words, and it helped me remember who I was and what type of life I wanted. Thanks to my bracelet, I ended up surviving a seriously boozy business dinner.

This bracelet that I had on my wrist with an inspiring quote and my sobriety date was a talisman. Talismans are defined as an object, typically an inscribed ring or stone, that is thought to have magical powers and bring good. I find talismans useful tools and reminders of my commitment to being alcohol-free, and they can also convey meaning to the wearer that may not be known to others.

Keep It Front and Center: Family Pictures, Affirmations, Talismans, and Tattoos

Below are some of my favorite symbols and talismans:

- Amethyst is a purple crystal, and the word comes from Greek, meaning "non-intoxicated" and is associated with clear thinking and sobriety. It can also be purchased in natural form and placed in your home as a reminder of your goal.

- Lotus flowers symbolize sobriety because the lotus flower grows directly out of muddy and murky waters to bloom and produce beautiful white and pink blossoms.

- Similarly, butterflies begin as caterpillars and transform through metamorphosis. I like the symbol of the butterfly because the caterpillar and butterfly are the same being, but through great internal cocooning, one becomes the other—an insect with wings and flight capability toward freedom to greater opportunities and food sources.

- Some AA meetings hand out chips based on milestones such as a month or one year. When a person receives a chip, it is typically given by their sponsor or a senior member of the community, and the chip receiver is asked to tell the group "How they did it." A chip is an achievement and symbol of honor. I have been in rooms where people have received ten-year, twenty-year, and even forty-year chips, and it is a standing ovation and full-court press moment for the receiver. It is customary for the chip to be passed around the circle for others to witness and be touched by the energy of the group. Many people cherish their chips and keep them displayed in their homes, while newcomers may keep their first chips close to them in their purses or wallets. A woman I know with many, many years of sobriety will "give back" her chips to members when they earn a particular milestone, because she feels that she will have no use for them once she is dead and wants to pass on all the wisdom and legacy earned from those chips.

Functional

- Trees, birds, and mountains are excellent symbols as well. I see a lot of tall and beautiful forest scenes on chips that symbolize growing strong roots and flourishing.

- If you subscribe to AA philosophy, you may notice a triangle symbol that characterizes unity, service, recovery—the three pillars central to overcoming alcohol addiction.

I do not have any tattoos. I view life as constantly changing and the reason is that if I cannot keep my hair color and cut the same for three years, I do not believe I can keep a tattoo for the rest of my life. That said, I know plenty of people who have gotten tattoos on their bodies. There's a phrase in sobriety: "Never Question the Decision." I first saw it in a book by Holly Whitaker about alcohol called *Quit Like a Woman*. Whitaker says when you decide to quit drinking, do not revisit the idea again, and never question the decision. The flip and flop of your mind back and forth to stop drinking and start drinking causes cognitive dissonance in your brain because you are not clear in the direction. I have come across people who have "NQTD," the abbreviation for never question the decision, tattooed somewhere meaningful on their bodies as a commitment to live a sober life.

I know a dancer who has an image of dancing on her shoulder that represents her freedom and an activity that enlivens and defines her. That tattoo reminds her of her focus on staying sober. Another fun tattoo is a comma, which people will get when they hit over one thousand days sober and are now part of the "Comma Club."

All these talismans, symbols, affirmations, and tattoos can serve as visual reminders of what your heart desires to feel, and they can be helpful as you work to keep your commitment. For me, they have served as reminders of home and intention, especially when I find myself in places and situations that distract or unbalance me.

Cravings, Urges, and the Law of Substitution

The most difficult thing about quitting drinking is dealing with the cravings. Functionals are used to working hard, putting on a good face, and solving problems. It is no wonder that we seek out comfort after we complete a hard thing or task. Early on when I stopped drinking, I would be fine during the day. I was used to getting up and going to work all day and not craving a drink, because I never drank at work. When I walked into my home and I was used to five-o-clock is wine-o-clock, I would experience an intense feeling of wanting to drink. My body and mind had grown accustomed to a wine habit, and my nighttime ritual was built around the satisfaction of a drink at the end of the day, which signaled that work was finished and the night was my time. As I took the first drink, dopamine was released, and I finally felt like I could relax. Dopamine is a powerful chemical, and my body and mind sought out that comfort daily to get that "feel good" hit.

If you want to be successful with being alcohol-free, you will have to address cravings. Good or bad, you have trained your mind and body that alcohol is a solution for stress and survival. *One helpful thing I learned about cravings is that they do not last forever, and they can be tamped down.*

Functional

Scientists have found that cravings typically last less than twenty minutes, and for me normally it is much less. You may need to distract yourself or sit with your cravings until they lose their power or control. You can survive for twenty minutes; it's not that long. In addition, most Functionals are used to delayed gratification, and knowing that the craving will only last for a twenty-minute stretch of time can help you push through the discomfort and anxiety until it is over.

Sit With the Craving

We think cravings come out of nowhere, but we have established habits or triggers that signal to our brain that alcohol soothes us. It is helpful to understand your triggers; this enables you to see your patterns. By recognizing those patterns, you can either choose to disrupt them or sit with the experience and do something different instead of giving in to the habit you are trying to break.

I live in Minnesota, a state that sees all four seasons. Summer means lakes, flowers, hot days, and shorts. Fall means gold and brown leaves, sweaters, and cooler weather. Winter means blankets of white snow, cozy throws, and nights by the fire. Every season is distinct and unique. I did not know, until I stopped, that the changing of seasons was extremely triggering for me. As a wine drinker, I tended to drink white wine because I did not like how red wine stained my teeth. I associated spring and summer with drinking white wine on patios, while fall and winter meant red wines inside. Whenever the seasons changed, I would be triggered or have a craving for the corresponding drink. Seeing women drinking wine at an outdoor café on a beautiful summer day, I would want what they were having, and I would know it was finally rosé or chardonnay season. Gradually, I would take in the scene and hold on to it for a second to "sit with the craving." Was that woman enjoying her rosé going to just have one glass or would she keep drinking more?

Would the few minutes of wine high be followed by depression or anxiety? Would she drink more than she wanted, and the bill would look blurry, and she would have to use extreme concentration to figure out the tip for the server? Would she stumble and wobble to the bathroom or slur her words?

After I contemplated the reality of the fanciful scene playing in front of me, I would pivot myself to my current life. I would think about all the benefits that living a life free of alcohol would give me: I was no longer a slave to anything. I did not ever have to have a hangover. I felt GOOD about myself. I felt invincible! Gradually, the patio scene lost its appeal because I started seeing the experience in totality. As that happened, the cravings began to lose their power.

Law of Substitution

Many times, it can be easier to alter a firm habit instead of completely changing it. Every day at about 5 p.m., the alcohol cravings would be fierce when I first stopped drinking. It was terrible and difficult. Logically, I knew it would take a while to establish a new pattern, but fighting the craving was excruciating and tough. I needed a way to alter some key factors in my nightly wind down experience instead of trying to have a completely different life.

Early in sobriety, I heard a podcast about a woman who put her nonalcoholic drinks in her wine glass on a nightly basis. She also purchased high-quality, organic juices, and justified her expense in these new purchases because it was "cheaper and healthier than wine." That logic worked for me. I began to fill my stemless, daily wine glass with sparkling water. I would go to the grocery store and explore an aisle that had been previously foreign to me. I would see all the fun sparkling water flavors—peach, cherry, lemon-lime—and buy up various options. I began to seek out mocktails, NA wines, and other alcohol-free alternatives. I would stock up my fridge and feel no guilt for all the NA options I had on hand to enjoy.

Miraculously, having these drinks available seemed to tamp down the cravings. The pattern now was Rachel gets home from work, Rachel pours a sparkling water into the pretty wine glass instead of wine, and Rachel drinks the NA drink as she cooks dinner. This action is called the "law of substitution." I was substituting a toxic drink for a nontoxic drink. I was keeping nearly the same habit loop, except there was no wine in my glass. There was a cue, sparkling water, and then a response. By replacing the wine with sparkling water, I changed the habit in a comfortable way. I'll admit it was a little uncomfortable at first, but I did get used to it, and indulging in my new drink of choice made it easier to stick to my goal.

A more dramatic way that I dealt with my nightly drinking habit by substitution was to submerge myself in water, literally. I used wine as a sleep aid, and early in sobriety I switched out wine for a bath. For many people, especially the high-functioning types, you might have drunk when you came home from work. For me, coming home from work meant that I was finished with my obligations and could relax and reward myself with wine. During those first few months of staying sober, I really needed something to do other than drink at night. I started by taking baths after dinner before I went to bed, because this was self-care that did not involve a hangover.

I also saw it as a hindrance to me driving to the liquor store. When you are surrounded by heated, luscious bubbles and your hair is wet, you are in no condition to get up and leave your house to go to the store. I do remember having wine cravings in the tub for no longer than twenty minutes, but the warm water washed them away, and I soon forgot about them. Baths before bed also calmed me and helped me sleep better. For years, I thought I could not get to sleep without wine. In fact, I was convinced of it. The baths calmed me and submerged me in a spot where I would not get out and pace my house seeking a drink. My bath became a nightly ritual, replacing a toxin with a positive habit, and helping me heal.

Give Yourself Lots of Rest and Support

Changing a habit such as drinking may be exhausting. When you start a new exercise regime, you may be tired because your body is not used to the activity. You will find your muscles fatigued or you may need extra rest because the movements you're going through are brand new. It is the same with giving up drinking. You'll find it hard at first and require extra rest and support. Plan accordingly for your first few days, weeks, and months. Plan for time to take a nap or have downtime. This will increase your likelihood of success and making this change for the better.

If you are trying to complete something hard and new, you also need to eliminate people in your life who are not supportive. The mom who always questions your decisions? She can wait for another day. The difficult home DIY project that will test your patience and fatigue your body? Save it for another day. Remember, you can always come back to these things later, but now your focus should be on eliminating the booze.

Time

The longer I stuck with my new habits, such as pouring an NA drink and taking baths, and the more successive days I went without a drink, the more the craving simply went away. I remember at six months realizing I had gone a full week without even thinking about alcohol. It did not cross my mind, and I felt free. I was so much calmer and more focused. I felt like myself instead of a wine monster. This is what moderation cannot provide: We never get permanently released from the power of our substance, and we cannot experience life independently from alcohol. Being sober and knowing you can stay sober is incredibly freeing, and you feel damn powerful no longer needing a substance. Just thinking about this makes me feel a rush of healthy dopamine.

Time away from the substance is extremely important. This is why all rehabs for alcohol and drugs require you to stay sober and avoid the substance entirely. The more days that you have away from your drug of choice, the less you crave the drug, learn to live without the drug, and return to yourself.

Time provides perspective and confidence. The more time I have without drinking, the more confident I get that I will never go back to drinking.

Functional

I never doubt it. It's not part of my life and it seems like a totally different life. Would I have thought that way after six months of not drinking? Heck no! I needed significant sober time to have a completely different life.

What Do I Tell the PEOPLE?

The law of attraction is a universal concept that states that you will attract into your life whatever you focus on. If you are a Functional reading this book, you likely find alcohol attractive and surround yourself with people who like to drink. Birds of a feather flock together. I remember looking through the pictures on my phone and seeing my friends during great moments of our relationship together, and we always had a drink in our hands or were attending a winery/brewery together. If you decide to drink less, take a break, or remove alcohol from your life, it is natural to wonder how you will get through a social situation or operate your life differently.

You may be used to walking into a social event and grabbing a drink immediately, and now friends or colleagues may notice that you are not drinking. You may have always been the life of the party, or your crowd of friends are all drinkers, and now different behavior may invite questions. You may feel you will be a social pariah or seen as boring. When I first took a break from drinking, I eliminated some social activities because I just did not know what to tell the PEOPLE.

Functional

I decided to take a break for one month, and I was feeling incredible for the first time in years. I was sleeping beautifully. I did not wake up with a hazy head. My stomach did not hurt. My eyes and skin looked bright and healthy. I felt alive and the most interesting I had been in years, since alcohol was no longer dimming my light. And I kept my promises to myself. That said, I had a challenging time expressing why I was not drinking or if I was going to stay sober. I was off in the corner listening to sober podcasts, reading books about quitting drinking, and meeting incredible people in recovery. It was such a niche experience, so different for me, and something no one I knew was doing. I mean, I had friends who traveled extensively, and they had unique experiences, such as visiting ashrams in Bali, but that was explainable. I could not quite comfortably tell people what was going on. I really did not have a story or explanation. I wrote this section to provide some helpful tips on what to say and not to say.

Be Proactive and Tell Those You Care About

If you are in a marriage or relationship with someone, have a close friend, or close family member, you need to let them know your plans. It is likely that they know you are struggling with drinking, even if you haven't discussed it with them, and it is also likely they will be supportive, at least initially. If they are close to you, it is likely they will understand you are trying to make positive changes. If they are drinking friends, this announcement will be impactful to them because drinking was an activity you used to do together. I like to set myself up for success and control the situation up front. You could send your friend or partner a text about not drinking. It may be more impersonal to do this over the phone, but it is also less stressful. You could state something such as "I am just giving you a heads-up that I am not drinking, but I am still excited to see you and hang out." When you are proactive, you are confident and strong, and respectful of the relationship. With this initiative-taking approach, you likely will have better results.

Pick a Phrase

The bullet points below offer some quick phrases that provide short and sweet reasons you are not drinking. In general, the simpler the phrase, the better. No one needs a long explanation, and you do not need to dwell or overexplain the situation. These phrases convey an intent, and the audience can ask more questions after you make your statement.

- "I'm not drinking."

- "I don't drink."

- "Yes, I will have a drink. Can I get a mocktail, 7 Up, club soda with lime, etc.?"

- "I'm alcohol-free." *I use this phrase often because I do feel like I am free of this addictive drug called alcohol.*

- "I do not drink. I am in recovery."

- "I'm sober."

- "Alcohol doesn't agree with me."

- "I'm the designated driver, so I am not drinking" or "I have to pick up the kids, so I am not drinking."

- "I have a fitness/wellness goal, so I am not drinking."

- "I'm not a fan of the taste or how alcohol makes me feel, so I don't drink."

- "I'm doing Sober September/October, Dry July, or an Alcohol-Free Month."

- My favorite expression lately is "Drinking lost its appeal for me," which absolutely feels true for me. It also challenges the belief that drinking is appealing to everyone, but once you remember the hangovers, woozy mind, diarrhea, and stupid things that you do when you drink, the activity becomes instantly unappealing.

*Notice I never recommend saying, "I am an alcoholic." The term *alcoholic* works well in a supportive AA meeting surrounded by similar people with a similar problem, but I do not believe it to be an empowering word when one is not in a recovery room. That said, if you like that word and you feel comfortable with it, go for it.

Beyond Your Close Friends or Spouse, It Is Likely That No One Cares

One of the most surprising things I discovered when I stopped drinking is that most people really do not care if you drink or not ... REALLY. People are mostly concerned about themselves and what people think about them. It is rare that an individual will focus solely on you and really care what is in your cup. I know that when I walk into a social situation, I do a quick mirror check to make sure that I look OK and do not have anything in my teeth, and I am conscious of whether my attire is going to match my surroundings. In other words, I am focused on myself and fitting in with the environment. People are generally selfish creatures and think about themselves.

It is rare that people ask me why I am not drinking. In the past six years of being alcohol-free, I have encountered this question in a social situation rarely. I have noticed that the people who ask me why I am not drinking fall into three camps: (1) They are asking because they have a problem, (2) I represent a mirror to them and it invites a question for them to change, or (3) they have a significant other with a problem

Beyond Your Close Friends or Spouse, It Is Likely That No One Cares

and they want information from me on how I did it or can help. I once ended up talking to a woman for about thirty minutes after casually saying "I wasn't drinking" in a group, and she spent time telling me all about her son and his drinking issues and asked about mocktails and support and everything under the sun.

The Art of the Pivot

Along the same lines that most people will not care that you are drinking, it may make sense to pivot the conversation to something else, especially if you are uncomfortable. For example, if you are new to being alcohol-free, you may not want to say more about the topic. You can turn the conversation back to your audience and ask them to speak about their latest vacation, their kids, their work, etc. If you want to redirect the conversation, you can always say, "That reminds me, I heard that you bought a new puppy. How is your family enjoying it?" and the conversation can shift to an easier topic. Remember, people love to talk about themselves and will always be flattered to hear that you want to know more about their lives. It is also acceptable to politely excuse yourself from the conversation and say, "Excuse me, I see Jane over there, and I need to talk to her about party planning. It was great to see you," and walk away.

Be Physical: Move Your Body

I want to circle back to the beginning of this section on planning and choosing two items that may help you successfully go alcohol-free. Being physical and getting exercise has significant health benefits, especially for those who are drinking too much. When we drink, our brains feel those pleasurable chemicals of dopamine and serotonin. We can get those same chemicals naturally when we exercise. When I say exercise, it does not have to be a 26.2-mile marathon. You can take walks or play pickleball. You can dance or swim with your kids in the pool. Functionals tend to embrace goals and achievement, and exercise can be a new and healthy distraction to focus on instead of drinking.

Exercise can also be great for coping with triggers and dealing with cravings. In an earlier chapter, I mentioned that scientists believe cravings only last twenty minutes. If you have the thought of driving to the liquor store, it can be helpful to take a walk for twenty minutes instead. You will find that you have removed yourself from an environment that may be triggering, such as your living room where you used to drink after work, and a change in scenery can shift your thoughts. When I have made myself go for walks, especially near nature, I notice things

Functional

like the tree branches swaying or funny birds that squawk. If I go on walks in the city, I might hear a street performer play chords on his saxophone to an upbeat song or notice the vibrant clothes that people wear in urban environments. Especially in early sobriety, I would take more walks or runs to deal with anger, boredom, and thoughts about drinking. I like to listen to podcasts or audiobooks when I walk and have found different sobriety podcasts that help me pass the time as I walk. By the time I finished, I was always in a better space from a mental health perspective than when I first started.

We know exercise can keep us at a healthy weight and body composition, but it also has great benefits for our mental health, especially if we consume alcohol. Alcohol is a depressant, and so it is not surprising that if you consume copious amounts you become sad and depressed. Alcohol also increases your chance of suffering from anxiety, and there is a pop culture term called "hangxiety," which describes the feeling of anxiousness that accompanies a hangover after you drink too much. By moving your body, you reduce stress and decrease anxiety and depression.

There are certain exercises and sports that cause you to focus intensely, such as racket sports and basketball, that can get you out of your head. Racket sports like tennis or pickleball force you to hit and return the ball based on a previous motion. You are constantly forced to adjust your reaction to make the ball go left, right, or down the center of the court to win against your opponent. Racket sports require strategic planning and decision-making, and it is hard to think about another thing such as alcohol when your brain is occupied by a ball flying toward you at high speed. If you were a social drinker and you missed the camaraderie of a bar with people, a pickleball court can be an easy place to meet others where the focus is not drinking. If you were a social drinker, a sport that is focused on people also invokes a principle shared in a previous chapter called the law of substitution: you can change up drinking friends with sports friends and get a healthier connection.

Exercise will help you with another problem that you will have when you go alcohol-free: time. In the last years that I drank, I was a daily drinker. I did not understand how many hours in a day it would consume for me to think about drinking, actual drinking, and recovery from drinking—even if I forced myself to complete things when I was hungover. Drinking often is literally a part-time job, and you realize that when you stop. Suddenly, I would wake up fully refreshed in the morning and productive. I would have endless energy and time that I did not have before. I was skipping happy hours, winery visits, and no longer planning for downtime after large drinking events. I could easily find time to take a yoga class, walk, etc. It was as if I gained a full few hours in my day.

Journaling and *The Artist's Way*

A woman in recovery raved about the Artist's Way Creative Cluster in which she was participating. The instructor was a yogi and was planning another offering. It sounded intriguing and now that I had stopped drinking, I had time for creativity. I wanted to write a book, and the *Artist's Way* process focused on "Morning Pages"—a dedicated writing practice of journaling your thoughts, ideally first thing in the morning. Every morning, I would write and find snippets of this book that you are now reading in my morning pages.

The Artist's Way is both a book and process that I highly recommend for anyone, regardless of creativity. The author, Julia Cameron, identifies as a recovering alcoholic, and the course is about contacting your authentic self and recovering your creativity. In addition to the daily practice of writing your morning pages, you also have artist's dates, which allow you to explore your inner child and provide self-care. The book provides a full twelve weeks of reading and exercises that facilitate a spiritual experience. I recommend that you purchase the book and companion workbook and do it yourself. I loved the process of completing the course with a group in a creative cluster. Once a week, about five or six women (all in recovery from alcohol) would meet to complete a weekly check-in where we would discuss the week's reading topic, such as connection or abundance, and share our findings from writing our morning pages and taking ourselves on artist's dates. As a corporate worker bee who creates PowerPoint decks and composes emails, I found this creative use of my writing exactly what I needed.

Now, many people might say, "I have no time for this!" That may be true, but the discipline of writing my morning pages did improve my life. I found myself creating my daily task list or expressing my rage for work or writing about a silly fight with my husband. Writing freely upon waking up enabled me to creatively channel my anger, so by the time I interacted with my day, I could approach it constructively and achieve better results. There have been many studies on the healing process of journaling, and I found the morning pages to be incredibly insightful and therapeutic, especially for those in recovery. A game changer, for sure.

Instructions for Morning Pages:

- Sit down every single morning and write down anything that comes to mind. Julia Cameron highly recommends that you complete this activity first thing in the morning every single day.

- Your goal is to get to three pages of writing. Some people use the written word as in three pages with a pen and paper. I use an app called Morning Pages because my handwriting is atrocious, but Julia Cameron prefers that you use pen and paper if possible. Adhering to this process partially helped me draft this book.

- Your writing can be utter nonsense. It can be epic poetry. Just do it and you will find that you start telling yourself things. If you write about your relationship with your significant other every single day, it is likely there is something to explore there. Your writing provides you with insight, taps into your aspirations and frustrations, and will help you process your feelings.

One Day at a Time

If I were to take my own advice and pick out a key item to work on that would make me successful for the long term, it would be to focus on the AA philosophy "One Day at a Time." Functionals are big thinkers and planners, and we tend to focus on the future. We review our relationships and can easily tell our children, employees, and business colleagues what to do because we apply lessons from our past experiences and challenges to our current problems. For example, we might think about the future and our daughter's wedding where we see ourselves toasting to the new couple with a glass of champagne or envision a crucial business dinner that absolutely requires a bottle of fine wine to win over the new client. We "future trip," and in doing so, prevent ourselves from seeing how an alcohol-free life could work.

When I began attending AA meetings, around Day 14, I heard this concept of One Day at a Time (ODAAT). Essentially, it means that we focus on just staying sober *today*. It means that when you get up, you think about your day. Will you be triggered to drink? Will your boss be their usually demanding self, and will you want to come home and drink away your tension and frustration? What do you need to stay sober today? Do you need to pack a better lunch/snack to keep your mood balanced? Do you need a meeting to connect with other sober people so you can commiserate and solve problems for an upcoming event at which you are scared you will drink? Do you need to detach from an interaction that is making you feel rage and simply go for a walk? All these are potential solutions to keep you from drinking and focused on addressing issues and living sober *in the moment*. Worry about tomorrow, tomorrow. Worry about today, today.

I often heard about One Day at a Time in AA meetings from people with a lot of sober time behind them. Someone with five years, ten years, or even thirty years of sobriety would stand up and receive their chip for the achievement of their major milestone. The meeting leader would ask them to tell the group what their story was and how they did it. Nearly every single one of them would say that they just took it ONE DAY AT A TIME.

So, what does One day at a Time really mean? It means only focusing on your day and not a lifetime. It means focusing on how to get through that tough meeting, sitting with a bad feeling instead of drinking over it, and taking small steps of progress. To stay focused on just THIS day seems easier than worrying about the rest of your lifetime. For example, when you think about not drinking, you might think of that next happy hour or baby shower or wedding and think, "Of course, I will drink then." That is a future trip, and it is not advisable. As you grow stronger and move further away from the drink, you forget how many days you are sober. You forget all the cravings and the past STRUGGLE starts to fade. Especially when you are first trying to stay sober, One Day at a Time should be your key strategy.

Hit the Pillow Sober

Along with the idea of One Day at a Time, you want to hit your pillow at the end of the day sober.

I remember having a dreadful day during my first year and thinking about drinking. The entire day, I received unwelcome news: My work project was not going well, and everyone was upset in meetings; my husband and I had a minor fight about something stupid, and when I told my friends about the work issue, no one seemed to care. My mood was crap, and I just did not see how the day was going to get better. I came home from work, poured myself a glass of sparkling water and moped around my house. Finally, I just put myself to bed at 7 p.m., because I was drained, in a foul mood, and just over it. I did one thing right that day: I hit the pillow sober, and that is truly the win when you have a drinking problem. The next day, I woke up after a beautiful sober sleep, I felt well rested, and I was much more clear-headed to tackle the day. My mood had shifted to more optimistic. Going to bed sober was all I really needed to do.

I see hitting the pillow sober like a video game goal. Your whole goal for the day is to hit your pillow sober. As you go through your day, you may see a friend you used to drink with, or you may pass a liquor store or see alcohol on the menu of a restaurant where you are eating with your partner. When you encounter those things, you are saying hi and bye to that friend, you are walking confidently by the liquor store without going in, and you are ordering a fun mocktail on the menu at that restaurant. You are bypassing all the obstacles to getting to the end of your day without drinking, without letting drinking control you. The strategy is to return to your home, alcohol-free, and hit the pillow at night without drinking. If you do that, your screen lights up with fireworks and you hear a delightful dinging of multiple points achieved as you win the game (for the day). This is what achievement looks like in sobriety. And here is the beautiful thing: The first days in sobriety are difficult because you are doing something new, just like when you are learning a new video game. You will be unfamiliar with the environment, you may take a wrong turn, or it may take you a lot longer to figure out what to order that is alcohol-free when you go to a restaurant for the first time.

After you gain some skills and play the game longer, this becomes effortless, and you easily hit your pillow at night sober. You become the gamemaster over time and it gets easier and easier to rack up points.

Counting Time

As a Functional, I would plan things around social events and work obligations, which also meant that I was planning out my drinking. I knew I needed to be careful about drinking when I went out or had to drive as well as plan around work events such as company picnics at which I normally did not drink or drank only one glass of wine. It can also be a wonderful thing to count your sober time.

It is a miraculous thing to have sober days. I remember having three days, seven days, and fourteen days without a drink. This was a big feat, especially since I was a daily drinker. For many women, the only significant time they will not drink is during their pregnancies after they discover they are carrying a child. For many adults, it can be agonizing just to think about racking up a full month without alcohol, so any stretch of not drinking is significant. As your stretch increases, your achievement becomes remarkable. As I have mentioned, I started to feel simply incredible, sleep better, and saw acne and stomach issues go away. You will want to also count the time for achievement as Functionals do for marathons and diets. It will feel good to rack up sober days, and I recommend it.

Counting Time

There are apps out there that can track your days. I use Nomo and the Recovery Elevator sobriety app. Each of the apps has a start date, and you can periodically check your dates. The Recovery Elevator allows you to have more than one clock in case you need to start over. It also counts how much money and calories you have saved, which was a large motivator for me over time. I was a person who immediately lost weight by ditching alcohol. Saving money became effortless as well. I used to spend about $1,000 a month on bottles of wine, going out for happy hours, getting an Uber, bringing over a host beverage, and getting a hotel room if I knew I was going to be drinking too much to drive. Over time, these expenses really add up.

At the time that I am writing this, I have an alcohol-free day count of over 2,400 days and over $58,000 USD in savings. (With inflation, I have saved much more.) Just think of what you could do with all that extra money! It could be a down payment on a home or the purchase of a nice car. It really is remarkable how your day count adds up over time, and you will want to keep track because it will make you feel good about having so many days alcohol-free. Speaking of money, I have had these daydreams as perhaps someone with my problem may have and they include someone offering me $1 million to drink again. It starts me down a funny path with the idea I could drink again and come back to sobriety, but I have met so many people who have not actually come back or tell me it is harder to get back than to just stay sober. I have decided I would not take $1 million—or more—to drink again, because I would have to essentially give up my peace, freedom, and confidence and that is too high a price to pay.

I do know people struggling to get sober, and they will count sober days even if they are not consecutive. This can work for people especially if they are struggling to get sober. You may not drink for three days and track those days in an app or notebook, but then you drink on the fourth

Functional

day and do not count it. Over time, people will realize they have more sober time in their year than previously. As you focus more and more on getting that clean time, you may look down at your count in a year and see that you have two hundred-plus days in a year that you have been alcohol-free and that is more than you have achieved previously by not counting and keeping track. Better is better, and it is something to be proud of.

In addition, counting and tracking can be comforting as a Functional because we do it in our occupations and real life to be successful. Accountants, financial advisors, personal trainers, mechanics, and business owners count time and progress. Even lawyers tend to bill in fifteen-minute increments. On a certain level, we know that we need to complete work and that time spent dedicated to a project counts. Stacking up those days and counting them signifies freedom from alcohol—you literally own your life, and a substance no longer dictates your outcome.

Sponsors, Therapists, Coaches, and Mentors

When I grew up, I played softball, volleyball, and ran track and field and cross-country. I was competitive and always wanted to do better. One of my favorite sports was cross-country, because I excelled at running at an early age. I remember being in sixth grade and having to run a mile for gym class and beat everyone (including the boys) in that distance. As I grew up, I had a cross-country coach named Dennis who watched us run and would give us feedback on our performance and suggestions for improvements.

Dennis was an excellent coach because he would focus on what I did well, such as keeping a consistent pace, but also told me to stop feeling like I needed to get out in front at the beginning. "Rachel, you do not need to assert yourself at the beginning of the race. Save that energy for the last part of the race and it will feel good to pass up others at the end. I know that it can be hard to conserve energy at the beginning but let us try this approach during practice and I bet you will benefit on race day." Dennis was correct. My time improved, as did my confidence

Functional

in passing opponents on the field and saving my lung capacity for the critical end of the race.

Like coaches on the field, there are experts who can help you figure out your blind spots. Many Functionals are used to being coached or are comfortable working in a hierarchical structure and understanding that there is a resource that can help them in the field. It can be beneficial to work with a sponsor, therapist, or recovery coach who can help you recognize your blind spots and guide you to a healthier path.

AA Sponsors

In most AA fellowships, sponsors are same sex; women sponsor women and men sponsor men. AA meetings are focused on the newcomer to sobriety. No newcomer must be sober, and I have been to plenty of meetings where people were not sober. The goal is to help people not drink. One of the tenets of AA is to have a sponsor, so generally each meeting will ask people in the room to raise their hand to signal if they would be open to sponsorship. In addition, there may be phone sheets or Google spreadsheets with phone numbers of people you can call or text if you need help, and those sheets will normally designate those people who could sponsor.

AA sponsors typically have at least one year or more of continuous sobriety and have an obligation to meet with their sponsee for step work. AA sponsors are someone you can call or text if you feel like you will drink or have questions about being sober. They are relatable to newcomers, and I do know many people who credit their sponsors for helping them stay sober.

My first sponsor was a woman I worked with in my first year of being sober. She was extremely outgoing and a big believer in AA and connected

Functional

me with several people. Unexpectedly, the major takeaway I had from her was around relapse. She told me that she relapsed at around six years sober, and it took her over a year to get back to the rooms of AA. She said that all of her old habits of blackout drinking, sleeping with strangers, and waking up in places she did not know and trying to find her clothes came back with a vengeance. She had been several years sober (the second time around) when I worked with her, and she was a vibrant woman who could be very accepting of parts of me I really did not want to expose or talk about. As a good sponsor does, she was available, and we completed the first eight steps of the twelve steps together. Her absence of judgment enabled me to talk more freely.

Another great aspect about her is that she introduced me to *The Woman's Way Through the Twelve Steps* by Stephanie S. Covington—a book about the twelve steps written specifically for women. *The Woman's Way* served as a better guide through the twelve steps than the Big Book of Alcoholics Anonymous (*Alcoholics Anonymous: The Story of How More Than One Hundred Men Have Recovered from Alcoholism*, nicknamed The Big Book) for me since it relates to women's lives exclusively. While there are stories about women in the Big Book, it was written in the 1930s and has several chapters that point to its male focus. (One of the few chapters that does not is called "To the Wives," which assumes that most alcoholics are men and addresses the wives who likely must handle the consequences and terrible behavior of the alcoholics.) My sponsor used *The Woman's Way* with me, and we attended a weekly women's Saturday meeting for a long time together. She was a long-standing member of the women's meeting, and I do believe that made it easier for me to integrate myself with others in the group and be invited to group hikes, movie nights, etc., which surrounded me with happy people who were sober.

In AA, there is also the concept of a temporary sponsor. The thought is that all sponsors are temporary, and you can work with a sponsor for as long as the relationship works for you. I did work with my first sponsor until I moved and after that, I worked with a sponsor who happened to work at the same company as I did in technology. We would periodically meet for lunch or just to get together. She was a woman with over twenty-plus years of recovery and married to a man in recovery. She had a lot of experience, and her presence was calming to me. When I met her, we discussed her being a temporary sponsor, but she became someone I met with periodically and trusted. Sometimes you might start working with a sponsor and perhaps your ideals or times to meet do not work for either one of you or you can move on to a different sponsor.

One major benefit of an AA sponsor is that anyone can walk into an AA meeting and ask for a sponsor and get help. AA really does not cost money (you are encouraged to donate a small sum for a meeting, but it is not required) and in capitalist America, it astonishes me sometimes that this organization has existed for so many years. Meetings and all AA groups are anonymous and are self-supporting with members who hold volunteer positions to welcome people to meetings, collect dues, and sponsor those who need help. There is an instilled responsibility in those who became sober for free sponsorship and that can be quite beneficial, especially because therapists and sober coaches cost money.

Another major benefit of AA sponsorship is that you work one-to-one with someone who had the same problem, whereas a therapist or recovery coach may have no practical experience or relatability to this issue. I found that the sponsors I had understood and looked out for situations that others without this issue may not have considered. For example, my earliest sponsor made sure that I went to weekly meetings and introduced me to several women in recovery. I was invited to walks and coffee events. She indirectly influenced my time in early recovery and suddenly I was surrounded by people in recovery instead of friends who drink, and that set me up for success. She turned out to be a good sounding board to discuss events with alcohol that I was nervous about attending.

Therapists and Recovery Coaches

So many people tell me they start a journey toward not drinking by interacting with and trusting their therapist to guide them. A therapist can be a safe place to begin discovery work. Do you have triggers or negative coping strategies that make you drink? Many therapists are trained in cognitive-behavioral therapy (CBT) and can work with you on identifying your triggers and working through everyday situations in a healthier manner. Therapists and counselors are professionals and have an ethical duty to help patients with their mental health and addictions, in contrast to AA sponsors who are mostly untrained volunteers.

For example, my AA sponsors were wonderful people but lacked a professional degree or certification to assess my relationship with alcohol. But a professional therapist may not always be helpful. I worked with one for a while after I was sober, and I had some discussions with her about drinking and staying alcohol-free. She was respectful and sympathetic, but she honestly did not "get it" as she did not struggle with drinking. I felt that my interactions with an AA sponsor were more beneficial because the sponsor could see through my "stories" and guide me toward an approach that was geared toward honesty and ownership. That said, this was just my isolated experience, and therapists can be a trusted and professional source for you to work on goals related to drinking or mental health issues such as anxiety, loneliness, or codependency. Since the pandemic, there are so many online apps that can easily connect you with a therapist such as Talkspace and BetterHelp, enabling you to work with a professional at your convenience in your own home.

Another option is a recovery coach. The recovery coach space is remarkably diverse, and there is not a one-size approach for how recovery coaches work with clients. Some recovery coaches work with clients who still drink, while others may not. A few of my friends have used SheRecovers coaches, who are women-focused, hold space, listen, provide accountability, and cocreate recovery plans with identified goals and personal growth. A friend of mine used a recovery coach who checked in on them daily through an app, and they felt that they could message if they drank or needed support. By working with a recovery coach, they had significantly more sober time this year than they'd had in their previous years, even though they are not completely sober. It is not a requirement, but several recovery coaches are in recovery themselves and have independent methodologies for connecting and working with clients. Some recovery coaches will offer specific group sessions, such as a Sober 90 group geared toward people in early recovery for their first ninety days or hold retreats for people in recovery or struggling with addiction.

Remember, the point of this section is to find one or two ideas that may work for you and think about how a person of influence could ultimately benefit you in accomplishing your goal and get you to a better place.

Sober Role Models

When you first begin a new lifestyle, you look for real-life examples of people who model what you want or are seeking. When I first became sober, I wanted to find my sober role models. I knew that Elton John was sober. Eminem, Bradley Cooper, and Macklemore were public about their sobriety, but what about sober women celebrities? I remember reading *Love Warrior* by Glennon Doyle and knowing she was sober.

Some sober celebrities did not exactly fall into the "rock bottom" category. I watched the 2020 Super Bowl and was shocked to learn that JLo, Shakira, and Demi Lovato mostly do not consume alcohol. JLo claims she did not drink for years because it ruins your skin. Shakira's brother was killed by a drunk driver and did not drink. Demi Lovato has had a long-standing fight with alcohol/drugs and her life was saved by Narcan, the emergency nasal spray used for opioid overdose. After the 2020 Super Bowl performance, where all three ladies KILLED it on stage with super energetic dance performances and the belly dancing prowess of Shakira, there were goddess-like images of them with the hashtag #soberissexy.

Blake Lively, a *Gossip Girl* actress, also does not drink. The *Sex and the City* gal Kristin Davis also does not drink and quit in college. Jada Smith admitted to stopping after she was drinking two bottles of wine on the couch at night. Gabby Bernstein, the manifestation guru, launched her career around the time when she quit alcohol and drugs. Kelly Ripa and Jessica Simpson are also off the booze.

One of my favorite sober celebrities is Bradley Cooper. He has been pretty open that he had issues with both drugs and alcohol because of his struggle with self-esteem. Cooper has acted in thirty-four different movies including *The Hangover*, *American Sniper*, and *Silver Linings Playbook*. One of my favorite movies that he directed and starred in is a rendition of *A Star Is Born* in which he plays an alcoholic musician who discovers and falls in love with a younger singer (Lady Gaga). The character he plays is so multifaceted: On the one hand, he is altruistic and kind and brings new songwriting talent along on his tour, and on the other, he is persistently drunk and publicly wets himself on stage, humiliating himself and his wife. *A Star is Born* was a captivating and raw performance by Cooper—even more so because you know he personally struggled with the same issues as the main character. He is vocal about not drinking and has explicitly stated that "Being sober helped a great deal with my rise in Hollywood." He confessed to Barbara Walters in 2015, "I would never be sitting here with you (if I did not change). I would not have been able to access myself or other people or even been able to take in other people if I had not changed my life" (Source: Bradley Cooper's Honest Quotes About His Sobriety, Getting Clean | usmagazine.com).

Here are some additional celebrities who count themselves as sober or do not drink:

- Supermodels Elle Macpherson, Chrissy Teigen, and Naomi Campbell

Functional

- Musicians Pharrell Williams, Florence Welch, Jack Harlow, Miley Cyrus, Lana Del Rey, Chris Martin, Jessica Simpson, Leona Lewis, and rocker Alice Cooper.

- Sports superstars like Brett Favre, Dennis Rodman, and soccer star Cristiano Ronaldo.

- Movie stars like Brad Pitt, Anne Hathaway, Zac Efron, and Drew Barrymore.

- Book authors such as Brené Brown, Matt Haig, and Stephen King.

It is empowering that these famous people tell us that their life does not include alcohol and how successful they are despite not consuming this drug that is advertised everywhere. Many people in this list are in recovery and have been vulnerable to the public and shared that they struggled with alcohol. As Bradley Cooper has stated, being alcohol-free has likely contributed to their success in their careers and boosted their professionalism.

Part III:
Deeper Dives on Key Topics

This next section is purely informational and may be of benefit to you and serve as a place to dive deeper into specific topics. The first topic that I will cover is what to expect in early sobriety from a mental and physical aspect. I group the information by how many days sober one would have. I wrote this book to provide knowledge to Functionals, based on concepts that I found helpful and what to expect by day count and the change that occurs when you put down the drink. This should help a reader understand what they experience in the early days of sobriety.

I also will dive deeper into AA, since it is the dominant recovery program in the United States, and possibly the rest of the world. I will give you my honest opinion and experience about being in the rooms of AA that

Functional

covers both the benefits and drawbacks of the program. It's clearly been a program that I benefited from and met several Functionals, but it is not my dominant method of recovery today. Within the AA sections, I also speak about the concept of anonymity and being comfortable with how much that you feel you should disclose about your journey. This topic was a large consideration for me, especially with a predominant leadership position and being a woman in a corporate environment. Finally, I discuss our relationships with people who still drink, especially our closest friends, spouses, or partners. These relationships can be some of the most important connections of our lives, and I provide advice and thoughts on how to relate and operate in those spaces.

Sobriety in Days and What to Expect in Early Sobriety

I started this whole thing with a dry September. Now, some people make fun of individuals like me who have a problem and decide to "take a break" like a dry month. They believe that it is not really addressing a problem, head-on, and instead the individual is making a pit stop on the way to denying a greater problem. That said, I personally am a fan of anything that gives people some sober time to figure things out. Simply put, people need time away from drinking to explore a new lifestyle. I do not know about you, but I could not even imagine going for three days without drinking. Even one month seemed unimaginable to me. Sober days get your brain out of the alcohol fog; they help you understand your negative coping mechanisms and experience your true self without poison. Another big benefit of taking a break is just getting good sleep to make decent decisions and seeing life clearly.

Here is a guide, based on my own experience, to what your first sober days might look like.

Functional

Day 0: You have contemplated quitting. You have told yourself that something needs to change, but quitting completely seems unimaginable. How exactly will one do THIS? Does it mean that you can't enjoy a drink on the patio? What will you tell everyone that you are doing? Day 0 is a tough place to be, but it is the step that happens before you decide to try Day 1 and before you create more days without drinking.

Day 1: You may be anxious. You might be hungover or have extremely low energy. You are trying to figure out what you do at witching hour. To prepare, I bought a bunch of sparkling water and put it in a pretty wine glass. I ate chips and went to bed early. I knew that I just needed to get it over with.

Many people in recovery refer to it as Day Won instead of Day 1, which is an excellent reframing of the situation. You are starting a new journey, and it is an important step forward. It is a definitive point forward, even if it is the first day.

Days 2 and 3: Like Day 1, but I personally felt more anxious these days. These three days are critical because you are not only not drinking but also detoxing from the alcohol in your system. Your body wants to replace that alcohol, which is why you crave it. Sweats could be common. You likely will sleep terribly and restlessly. I remember a low-grade headache, which was likely a symptom of withdrawal. I remember the cravings that seemed like a background song throughout the day. I felt a whole lot of discontent and I didn't feel like eating. I remember pacing around my house and the general feeling of restlessness and unease.

On a positive note, nothing in my first three days was worse than a hangover. Not even a little bit. I mention that because I was very worried about detoxing and my fears turned out to be unfounded, even though I was drinking about two bottles a day. It may be helpful to take a walk and keep your schedule light on these days and understand that your mind and body will be "off" the first few days.

Day 3: I am sitting in our kitchen with my husband eating dinner, which we do every single night together. It is Day 3, and I have not told him that I am not drinking. He looks over and does not see my wine glass and asks, "Hey, are you not drinking?" "Yes," I say slowly. "I am not drinking."

At the time, I was reading a book called *This Naked Mind*, which is a book about giving up alcohol. I told him about the book and my audacious goal to be sober for one month. I told him that this is Day 3, and this is the longest I have gone without drinking for several years, maybe seven years? I tell him I am really scared, but I am really going to try. My track record (as he knows) is not good. But I am serious this time. I am trying.

He listens and tells me he will fully support me. It seems like we know that this is different from the last few times when we discussed my drinking. In those discussions, I was defensive, and I didn't really see it as a problem, or at least a problem that I needed to quit entirely. In the past, all my attempts were moderation-based, such as only one glass of wine or drinking only four days a week. This time, however, I am vulnerable in stating my goal to not drink for a month. I tell him that I am trying out a month without drinking. I also say under my breath that "it could be longer." He hears that and he takes it in. Wisely, he knows not to press for more information or promises that I will keep to the month. We sat together, but in silence.

Days 4 and 5: I am a little giddy. This is the longest that I have gone without alcohol. I had a happy hour with an open bar. For those who ask, I tell them that "I am doing Dry September." I had rehearsed this excuse and figured that it would "pass muster." I also was partially in charge of hosting it, because it was related to a celebration of a deal

Functional

that our teams had closed with another financial services firm. No one really inquires much about it and for that, I am relieved.

Days 6 and 7: These are the treasured days, because beautiful and precious sleep comes to me. Oh my gosh, it is wonderful. I will honestly call this Oscar-worthy sleep, and my body just loves it. I felt like I haven't slept this well in years and I can't stop smiling. I recall about a year before when I went to the doctor and complained about my sleep. My Mayo Clinic-trained doctor had provided me with a lot of advice, such as blackout blinds, no blue light tech devices before bed, and also said that I should limit alcohol consumption when I complained that I didn't feel well rested. That said, I had no idea just how much alcohol impacted my sleep quality until I slept this well on about day 6. It was a night-and-day difference.

Also, I jumped on the scale. I magically was down six pounds! What?! I have a smaller frame, so six pounds is dramatic. My wedding ring feels loose, and I feel less bloated.

Between the weight loss and the beautiful sleep, I feel surprisingly optimistic. Perhaps, I can do this sober month.

Days 7 to 13: I am still so curious about sobriety. I listen to some sobriety podcasts, such as *Home* with Laura McKowen and Holly Whitaker and find other podcasts like *Recovery Elevator*. I hear people on the podcasts who sound just like me: hardworking people who have this problem that drives their spouses crazy, and they hide bottles just like me. I start to think that I am not so alone in this problem. These people have a longer sobriety time than I do, and they tell me how happy they are and that they feel they are living now. I still do not quite understand how they operate in normal life without drinking, but I keep listening.

Sobriety in Days and What to Expect in Early Sobriety

I hear guests who talk about attending AA. They do not seem like losers. They appear to be ordinary people. I start to consider that I should try out an AA meeting. Also, during this time, my husband checks in with me in little ways. He asks me if I am having cravings and if I am OK. I tell him that I am going to stock up on sparkling water, which seems kind of silly. It is expensive water with bubbles, but we both acknowledge it is a less destructive and less expensive option than wine.

Day 14: It is a Saturday, and I am attending my first AA meeting. I tell myself that it is just like going to a new spin class or a yoga studio. I just must try it out for an hour. I might find no value or think everyone is a worse-off person than me. I mean these people could be so bad that maybe it would mean that my little experiment should stop—and I am not an alcoholic! I go to the AA meeting about fifteen minutes away from my house with judgment and await my assessment that I am "not like these people." I go to a women's meeting, and everyone is nice and welcoming—not what I expected. The meeting organizer asks us to go around, say our name, number of days sober, and if we are new to this meeting. I hear the other women speak and they all say some version of "Hi, I am Ann. I am an alcoholic." I speak. "Hi, I am Rachel. I am an alcoholic. I am fourteen days sober and new to this meeting." I really just spoke the verbiage, because everyone else did it. I did not know it then, but a small number of days sober signals to others that they should make sure I know about resources, and they help me out in the meeting.

We break up into small groups and a woman tells me that she will do a "1st step" meeting with me and asks her friend to join our group. I tell them I am trying to figure out if I have a problem or not. I tell them that I drink daily, but I am super high performing. I tell them I have not had these negative consequences like DWI or job loss.

Functional

One of them corrects me. "You haven't had it—yet." She explains that she used to think she wasn't that bad either, until she received a DWI and ended up in treatment. Her words sunk in. When she talked, I could tell she was educated and seemed to have an excellent job. I started getting a little emotional and tearing up a little. My experiment was failing: These people were like me. They all gave me their numbers and one even made me type her number into my phone. The meeting ended and they said, "Keep coming back."

Day 30: Within the first month, I was pretty sure that I was experiencing the Pink Cloud. A pink cloud in sobriety is a euphoric bliss or a high point that comes when you cease drinking. It could be physiological, meaning that when you stop injecting an addictive poison, your mood, health, and outlook on life improve. It could be aroused from a sense of accomplishment: I was conquering a bad habit, and every day ensured that I was winning at my goal. I know that sober sleep and seeing the world clearly and without a low-grade hangover produced inner peace.

In the first month, I was also very curious about this sober new world and the people in it. I listened to tons of podcasts and interviews to hear people like me. One of my favorite podcasts is *Recovery Elevator*. The hosts interview "regular" alcoholics and ask them this funny interview question: "You might be an alcoholic if you ..." The answers made me laugh for days and I related. You might be an alcoholic if you hide your bottle under the couch and hear the "clank" of that bottle against your other bottles. You might be an alcoholic if you go into your regular liquor store, and they see the twenty-four bottles of wine that you are buying for yourself and ask if you are having another party? These answers are HILARIOUS because they are true, and I would listen to these responses and laugh my foolish head off and not feel so alone in the world that some bloke in the UK did the same stupid shit that I did because we both had the same problem.

Sobriety in Days and What to Expect in Early Sobriety

In the first month, I remember being very concerned about whether people would know that I had a problem, and I wondered if they would treat me differently. I was so concerned about THE PEOPLE. It is good to read advice from others who are on this journey or talk to a trusted friend. My husband is nearly a nondrinker, and I would tell him all my worries and we would plan what I could do to make social situations easier. He didn't totally understand everything that I was going through, but it really helped having an ally.

For me, the cravings were the worst in my first month. I would walk in the door of my home after work, the time when I used to immediately pour myself a glass of wine—and I would begin salivating. I would drive by a liquor store and find my mind creating a picture of the exact shelf with my favorite brand of chardonnay or pinot grigio. It seemed like the cravings were a large monster that would be unexpectedly activated by simply doing nothing. Despite these distractions, I did not want to go back on my one-month promise of not drinking and besides, my sober sleep was so incredible that it kept me grounded and committed to my goal.

At the end of the month, I did know if I would stay sober for the rest of my life. I did know that I was onto something, and I felt physically good and proud of myself. I decided to keep going. I also realized that I was incredibly thirsty for knowledge about sobriety and people who did not drink. They seemed to know something that I did not.

Day 60: In my second month, I started attending more AA meetings. I did not know what to think about AA at first, but these people seemed to have a plan and proof that the plan worked. I would meet people with years of sobriety who were happy, successful at their jobs, had happy relationships with their partners and were good parents.

Sometimes, I would meet these perfect people in the rooms of AA, and I would stare at them and ask them if they really were bad off before they stopped drinking. They would laugh and tell me lots of great stories about homes lost, jobs that they could not hold, etc. It almost was unbelievable. I remember talking to a woman in a meeting who seemed super put-together, kind, established and happy. I commented on these noticeable attributes, and she told me that she had struggled for two years to get sober and kept relapsing in her tiny apartment but went to meetings and kept getting better. I never would have guessed that when I looked at the perfect human specimen standing in front of me. The cool thing was just how helpful and humble she was, and how she told me to keep coming back.

I also noticed the people at meetings who kept drinking. Now, sobriety support meetings are spaces for people to come to get sober. All one must have is the desire to stop drinking. I would observe fellow humans with this issue week after week who did not stop drinking stay stuck in their problems. A guy who kept drinking would complain about his wife who nagged him about helping with their kids. "Why didn't she just get off his back?! Why did she expect him to pick up kids from sports or school?!" Both he and his wife worked, but school and sport pickups clearly cut into his drinking and TV time.

Meanwhile the other guy in the group, who also had kids, but had gotten sober, would report back that he was responsible and present to be a father and his relationship with his wife was the best it had been in a long time. I began to see the stark difference in people week after week. It was like those who kept drinking just stayed stuck. I respect progress, and I was witnessing week after week in these meetings that there were those who were starting to obtain a happy life with successful relationships, jobs, and a smiling and relaxed demeanor, and those who kept drinking with the same negative results who were unproductive and stagnant.

Around two months into sobriety, I started working with an AA sponsor. It happened like this. I attended a regular AA meeting, and a friendly and vibrant woman talked to me after a meeting and asked me if I needed a sponsor. I told her I wanted to think it over—and I did think it over for a week. I just really did not like being vulnerable with another human, but I decided that having more sober influences in my life would not be a bad thing. At the end of the week, I asked her to be my sponsor, and we started working the steps.

In hindsight, this was quite beneficial to me because I was able to interact with another woman in long-term sobriety on a personal level. My sponsor had several years of sobriety, even after a painful relapse. She also had an established group of sober girlfriends and had a sense of lightheartedness. She seemed to have ease with the present moment and could listen and easily interact socially with several different kinds of people. One thing that she had me use for our sessions was a book called *The Woman's Way Through the Twelve Steps* by Stephanie Covington, which breaks down the famous AA steps from a feminine perspective. I found it to be relatable and trusted the content more than the traditional AA Big Book, even though they both share the same principles. It was my way in.

Another aspect of working with a sponsor was that it kept me busy and provided another sober environment. All this new information was flooding into my previously alcohol-influenced brain, and I was consumed with a thirst for knowledge on everything related to addiction. Besides AA, I did join an online recovery group called Recovery Elevator, which had amazing people and wasn't spiritually focused like AA. These two programs balanced each other out, because they are quite different in the sense that Recovery Elevator doesn't have a program and is just for people trying to get and stay sober.

Functional

Also, around two months I began to look healthier, and some of my friends would ask me what new beauty product I was using. I was sleeping well, and my skin looked like a Cover Girl commercial—bright and glowing—and even my wrinkles seemed diminished. My eyes no longer had a faint yellow tint, and a weird rash I had for ages that no rash cream could get rid of just disappeared. My nails looked strong and healthy, and the tips were white. My stomach was no longer bloated, and all the constipation and diarrhea associated with drinking were gone. My hair seemed to have more luster.

I also felt great! If I could describe it, it seemed like I was five to seven years younger. I had more energy and stamina. I could concentrate better. It seemed effortless to work out and handle more issues at work. It even seemed that my posture had improved, and I was standing taller. If I could summarize this feeling, I would say that I had a feeling of better well-being.

90 Days: After around three months—ninety days—I started to think that I was "cured" of alcoholism. I mean, I had gone ninety days without drinking, which seemed like an eternity. That must mean I could drink again, right?! I tell my husband about this thought, and he becomes really quiet and hunched over, and I rapidly start to discuss what it means, such as maybe I only drink on weekends or at special events. He is stays incredibly silent and finally says, "Maybe you should go to a meeting and talk about it with your group." So, I go to my Monday night AA meeting and tell the group everything that I have been thinking. I tell them that with my previous drinking, that I hadn't lost a house, a job, and didn't lose my relationship. I remember saying the words: "Maybe I am not an alcoholic and maybe I can drink again!" The people who have heard me talk about my drinking for a few months stare back at me and the more seasoned people in the group step up to share. It was as if I activated the old-timers in our group.

Sobriety in Days and What to Expect in Early Sobriety

A guy tells me a story of how he had that same thought at around ninety days sober and the next thing he knew, he was at the bar drinking his usual drink and ended up driving down the freeway in the wrong direction and ended up in jail. He said that it turned out to be the best thing because he went to an AA meeting in jail, started working the steps, never drank again, and ended up in the nice suburb where we all were right now attending this AA meeting. This was not exactly the story I wanted to hear. After the meeting, a super punk rock, assertive woman I was a little afraid of approached me. She was three years sober and told me that it was natural at ninety days to be thinking about going back to drinking. She said other things that resonated, and then she spoke directly to my achiever/perfectionist self. She said, "You know, if you drink again, you have to start your clock all over again."

That stopped all my thoughts about returning to drinking for the moment. I had never considered that I would have to give up my day count and I had worked hard at getting those days. I also received a few sobriety chips and claps and congratulations for making it past certain days. I felt successful and I liked feeling successful (as a good Functional does). I immediately realized that being back on Day 1 again would feel like a total defeat and I wasn't ready to give it up, at least not now. I knew after that conversation that I wasn't going to drink any time soon. I didn't want to go backward. Therefore, I stayed sober. I am eternally grateful for that conversation, and I told her that later. It was a key moment when I needed straight talk, and I needed someone to address exactly what I was thinking, and she gave it to me. Her honesty helped me stay alcohol-free, and I can't think of another person such as a therapist or even my husband who could have given me that key conversation. And so, I stayed sober.

Day 100: When I hit triple digits, it felt huge. My self-confidence was bursting, and I'd been sleeping soundly for a solid three months. At

Functional

around one hundred days, our emotions stabilize. I stopped crying, which had only started up when I got sober. I found out that your hormones finally stabilize around ninety to one hundred days. I finally believed this sobriety thing might be more than a phase, and I began to visualize how a permanent change in my life would look.

My one-hundred-day mark happened to be around Christmas and New Year's Eve, which is a large drinking season filled with work and holiday parties. I skipped out on all the boozy events and made excuses for the usual annual get-togethers because I just felt like I didn't want to deal with it. I didn't know what to say and still felt awkward and conflicted in drinking situations. It was a little difficult to tell people that I could not attend an event, but at the same time, I noticed I was truly taking care of myself physically, mentally, and spiritually. I cocooned myself at home and my nights were composed of drinking sparkling water instead of wine. I spent my time going to work, meetings, and participating in my online world of recovery.

Another thing that I will mention about this ninety-to-one-hundred-day period and mood stabilization: Alcohol may actually be your problem and not depression or anxiety. People would tell me they were on medications for depression and anxiety while drinking, and after they became sober for one hundred days and their mood stabilized, they realized they did not have the mental health condition they thought they had. It's hard to know what one's core issue is until this toxic depressant is removed from your system first.

100+ Days and Into Your First Year of Sobriety: There is a saying in AA that in your first year of sobriety, you should just focus on being sober and make no major life decisions. The advice is: Do not get a divorce, leave a job, start dating, or start a major new project. It is hard enough just to stay alcohol-free, especially for someone who has likely spent years drinking. One may be tempted to erratically quit a job or leave a marriage, when they are just establishing themselves in a new life. There is a lot of truth and wisdom in this advice. For me, my cravings and old patterns of thinking came up with a vengeance in the first year when there were holidays or other social events where I would normally drink. For years, my coping mechanism for stress and anxiety was alcohol, and I was used to hiding my drinking while remaining as a Functional, so I felt vulnerable that first year, because I had to do my life without my security blanket. That said, however, I realize how wonderful that first year felt because I felt powerful in not succumbing to a drink and really taking charge of my life.

For the first year, I did skip out on social events that just seemed too overwhelming. Staying away from drinking and doing something entirely new can be extremely draining. I skipped my eighty-person Christmas party at my mom's side. It was an annual tradition, but I just did not want to see all the wine bottles and people holding wine glasses. I did not want to have to explain myself and I didn't want to be trapped in a situation where I could not easily leave. So, I stayed home and drank my fizzy water, read a book, and snuggled next to my cats. It was a good Christmas.

One Year Sober: At one year sober, I knew that being sober was my new lifestyle. I also felt proud of myself. I had not drunk in one year. For my one-year anniversary, I planned to go out to a hip, bubbly restaurant that I read served great mocktails. I reflected on the year, and I remembered how much I had changed and how I'd stayed present—and sober—even when things seemed hard. I had a weekly women's AA meeting that I attended, I had a good online recovery community, my marriage was improving, I was newly promoted in my job, I had lost about thirteen pounds, and my skin and eyes were glowing. On my one-year anniversary, lots of people in my small recovery world gave me accolades and congratulations. I felt happy and successful. I was forty-two and at one year sober, I felt like I had made a comeback. *Cue the boxer ring walk-out song.*

My AA Experience

You really cannot talk about heavy drinking in America without talking about Alcoholics Anonymous (AA). I wrote this chapter to provide a lens into this organization. I meet people who are absolute proponents of AA and believe that there is no other recovery program out there, as well as the exact opposite—people who believe it is a brainwashing cult of yesteryear. I would like to just speak about my experiences and thoughts on the topic. I do recommend everyone try out a meeting or two to see what you think about it, but if it doesn't resonate, try something different.

AA started in 1935 in Akron, Ohio, with a meeting between Bill W., who was a New York stockbroker, and Dr. Bob, a physician. Both men suffered from what they deemed to be alcoholism. (I was always drawn to the fact that Bill W., one of the founding fathers of AA, was a stockbroker, because I work in financial services and am also licensed as a stockbroker.)

Both Bill W. and Dr. Bob were influenced by an Episcopalian spirituality called the Oxford Group, and as they became sober, they spent time in the Akron City Hospital working with alcoholics and trying to get them sober. I find it fascinating now, but many people suffering from alcohol use disorder had no treatment or rehab and would simply end up at the hospital because neither they nor their families understood how to deal with their condition. As the men spent time together and with other men suffering from alcoholism, they discovered a key component of their recovery was working with another alcoholic, which has become a foundation of AA's program. There is a saying in AA that AA is not a "me" program, it is a "we" program. AA is structured around recovering alcoholics sponsoring those trying to get sober and completing service for the organization, such as making the coffee at a meeting or organizing spaces to meet.

While I came to AA fully as a human suffering from a drinking problem, I must talk about it as a global and far-reaching organization. My lens is that of a businessperson working in a capitalist environment, and I find it impressive that AA operates in over 180 countries with 2 million members and 118,000 groups. There are thousands of meetings online and in person, and yet there is no real financial backing. And yet, at any time of day, a person suffering from alcoholism can find a meeting or perhaps call a local number and speak to someone. An AA tenet is that AA takes no money from outside sources to protect influence and all meetings must be self-sustaining, which means there may be a collection cup passed around to maintain rent for the meeting space or request for an online payment. Most times, the Big Book of Alcoholics Anonymous is given out for free to newcomers. Contributions are not required, and I have never attended a meeting where there was pressure to aggressively donate; people generously offer their support financially or by volunteering for various acts of service.

While I primarily attended meetings in the cities I have lived in, I have also attended meetings while traveling for work or vacation in other parts of the globe. The principle of the meeting is similar wherever you

Functional

go, and everyone greets you like a friend. When I traveled to Miami, the land of beautiful clubs and bars with fancy drinks, I went to a meeting when I first arrived. The meeting was women-only and met at a church. When I arrived at the address, I expected to descend into a dingy basement of a rundown church. Instead, the church was a gorgeously preserved Spanish-style building with stunning architecture. As I walked to the part of the grounds where we were meeting, I passed courtyards with tree branches on which hung beautiful dream catchers. I entered the women's meeting and told them I was less than a year sober, from out of town, and that the bar across the street from my hotel looked too tempting when I arrived. The women welcomed me and hugged me like family.

One woman gave me advice on restaurants that served incredible nonalcoholic drinks and shared discounts on amazing local gardens and museums, as well as her phone number to use while I was there. This was a perfect stranger who met me in a meeting and understood I was only there for a week and a little shaky in my sobriety. I would not be an invested person in her life, and yet she made me feel secure about an unfamiliar environment and set me up for success. After that meeting, I had no cravings for the endless bars that dominated Miami and my sneaky thoughts about "I'm on vacation and should be drinking" simply disappeared. All I had done was attend a free meeting with people like me and meet someone who took time to check in with me in a city with which I was unfamiliar. The generosity of AA and its people has never ceased to amaze me.

AA's premises are centered on being anonymous and it is a principle outlined in the Twelve Traditions. This principle of anonymity is said to have immense spiritual significance. Being anonymous, those who have a problem and want to get better have a safe space to meet with others who share a similar problem. It also protects the organization in the event a member "goes off the wagon," drives drunk and potentially causes someone harm, which could in turn create public scrutiny of AA. In meetings, people generally share their first name and/or their last initial. For example, the founding father of AA is Bill W. Members may not identify themselves publicly or on social media. There is a phrase used in AA that says, "What is said here, stays here." And then the room participants echo, "Here! Here!" That phrase expressed in the rooms of AA means that you can speak openly about your experiences or struggles, and you are in a space that will not publicly disclose your wrongdoings.

While there are a great many benefits of remaining anonymous, especially if you are still drinking and seeking help or are new in sobriety, there may be longer-term consequences of keeping yourself and your problem hidden. For someone struggling, it is important to see people modeling a sober lifestyle and being happy, free, and overcoming addiction. Also, social media has really changed mental health and addiction struggles; it is more acceptable now to be out and open about alcohol use disorders. Recovery is celebrated on Facebook, Instagram, and TikTok when someone shares a significant day count, such as one year of being alcohol-free. While AA does mandate being anonymous, I believe that both being anonymous in a meeting setting where confidentiality and trust are critical, as well as being public about celebrating sober time and lifestyle can coexist. After all, conquering challenges and overcoming adversity make for a beautiful, human story that can be both incubated and protected, as well as told when the time is right.

My opinion about AA before I had ever entered a room was that this was the place for the worst of our kind with a drinking problem. I imagined that I would see only nonfunctional, drunk people who could not hold a job, like that stereotypical homeless guy living under a bridge with a brown paper bag. To my great surprise, I met lawyers, principals, extremely

Functional

wealthy businesspeople, and even celebrated TV personalities in the many AA meetings I attended. You soon realize that addiction touches all socioeconomic classes, religions, races, genders, etc. I have met several Functionals in the rooms of AA, and they tend to be well put together and successful, with good jobs and family lives. Even with all that, they can have immense struggles with alcohol with DWIs, rehab stints, lost jobs, and family members who suffer from their drinking. Alcohol use disorder does not discriminate.

The other item to mention about AA is that it was founded by men who were Christian, and in meetings you will often hear people talk about God or say the "Our Father" prayer. I grew up in a religious environment, so this god was a familiar concept for me. But this aspect of AA may not sit well for everyone. It is important to note that AA does recognize agnostics and religions other than Christianity, and the Big Book will use the term "Higher Power."

When I was new to sobriety and in AA rooms, I was told about this concept of Group of Drunks (GOD). Group of Drunks refers to your group in AA comprised of elders with several years of sobriety, people in meetings trying to remain sober, and the newcomer who needs help. When you sit in an AA circle, you actually feel this presence of the Group of Drunks, aka God, because you feel safe and with your people and that it is good and you are loved. I grew up Catholic and spent time in churches and with nuns, priests, and other spiritual people, but I have never felt the presence of a Higher Power more clearly than in an AA circle. In AA, you see perfect strangers helping perfect strangers with a shared problem. You hear stories about how other alcoholics overcame this addiction to tell others, so that newcomers know there is a path, and that success is real. For me, I may disagree with religious institutions of God, but I could get behind Group of Drunks, and it is still the belief I carry today as my meaning of a Higher Power, especially as it relates to sobriety.

My AA Experience

My favorite part of AA is the fellowship. When you walk into a meeting in person or virtually, you are greeted and welcomed. The focus of the meeting is the newcomer, so those who are struggling can get help, such as a meeting schedule or a sponsor. When you attend a new meeting, they do like to ask if people are in their first thirty days or new at the meeting, because they want to welcome you and make you aware of the resources available and connect you with a sponsor. I have gone on lengthy hikes, joined coffee meetups, and attended sobriety celebrations with people I met in AA. The fellowship extends beyond your local meeting, and I have met so many incredible AA people in the craziest of places, such as bars (yes, bars), airports, elevators, and even work who have become instant friends once we shared our common path. A Stanford researcher found that AA fellowship helps more people become sober than traditional therapy after evaluating thirty-five studies of 10,080 participants. The researcher found that the program worked because of all the support members offer each other as well as tips to stay sober. This stat makes sense to me. I find myself listening to and trusting the advice of a person with a longer stretch of sobriety than I have because I know they have experience and are authentic as opposed to someone who may have simply studied addiction (Source: Alcoholics Anonymous Most Effective Path to Alcohol Abstinence | med.stanford.edu).

Despite the positivity I feel about AA, there are some things that I struggle with. For example, I love using the term *alcoholic* in an AA meeting, but outside the rooms, it is misunderstood and used negatively. In addition, alcohol is an addictive drug, class one carcinogen, toxin, and depressant and is terrible for everyone: not just "alcoholics." And beyond the physical damage it causes, alcohol is harmful to anyone who drinks because our culture presents—and markets—drinking as normal even though alcohol is a destructive drug. AA does not recognize that alcohol is a bad substance or that alcohol companies have any fault in the selling of this harmful drug. It squarely focuses on the individual, using personal responsibility instead of accessing the full picture of how modern addiction theories are understood. Alcohol is classified as a medically addictive substance. Everyone who drinks has the potential to become addicted. In AA, the language used is contrasting: There are alcoholics and there are "Normies," or those who can drink "normally." The spectrum of addiction just doesn't support this information and this program ignores science.

In addition, I don't love how the Big Book is focused mostly on white, cis men, as this makes it difficult for me to connect with the stories and vernacular as a woman living in the 2020s. I also do not love that only AA literature is used in meetings because it limits outside and inclusive content that may resonate with people. I have also met people in AA who are rigid and seem almost like religious fanatics. The best advice I have gotten for dealing with these aspects of AA is another AA saying: "Take what you want and leave the rest." I find that if I attend an AA meeting and some aspect may not be in alignment with my values, I notice it and set it aside. I liken it to going to a foreign country: there can be customs and traditions that may not be understandable to you, but you can be kind and respect their intent and their history.

Today, AA is not my primary or even secondary method of staying in recovery. I normally attend an online sobriety support meeting quite often that chooses to use readings from all distinct kinds of books. Some of the people who attend and run the group are in AA, but many are not. The group's focus is sobriety, but it does not offer a program like the Twelve Steps. It has a local subgroup that I meet up with once a month in person for coffee or art festivals. I like the primarily online setup because it fits my busy lifestyle, and I can access it whenever I need a meeting. That said, I occasionally attend an AA meeting in person and recognize that they offer support for free to millions of people, and there is something special about being in an AA room with people who struggle with the same problem.

Some questions to ask yourself:

- *Would trying out an AA meeting make sense? If so, what type of format would be best for you: in-person, online, women only?*

- *Do you know anyone who has been or is a part of AA? Do you know what their experience was? Would you feel comfortable asking them about it?*

- *If you are reluctant to attend, why is that? Is there another program that may fit your lifestyle and spiritual preference such as SMART recovery, The Luckiest Club, or Recovery Dharma (recovery program based on Buddhist principles)? If this chapter does not resonate and you know that AA is not for you, know that it is perfectly acceptable as well.*

Being Out as Sober/Alcohol-Free: It Is YOUR Choice

As a person who used to have a drinking problem, my biggest fear used to be how it would end up influencing my professional life. A convincer on why I needed to change my drinking had to do with waking up in the morning and thinking that a drink would be great before work. The "hair of the dog" is a proven remedy for helping you feel better after a hangover. That thought in my head of having a drink before work terrified me—and I never did.

Instead, I used to punish myself every morning and tell myself that it was my lack of control that was the problem. I was bad and needed to "figure it out." I never shared the problem with anyone outside of a few girlfriends I knew were heavy drinkers. If I had shared my problem with people who were successfully sober, I'm confident that I would have received better guidance.

My drinking problem was shameful, and it did not fit my otherwise "perfect life." Especially professionally, I was overly concerned with anyone thinking I had a problem. When I first started joining recovery groups online or attending AA, I was incredibly worried that people that I worked with would be in meetings. But I needed to get better and figure out how to handle my drinking more than I feared people. Thankfully, AA is anonymous and those who had a problem would not want to broadcast that they had seen me at an AA meeting, not only because it would implicate them but also because it would violate AA's code.

I was not a person who "recovered out loud," at least not initially. As I mentioned earlier, my initial goal was just not to drink for a month, and I kept going because I felt incredible and more like myself and being alcohol-free worked so well for me. I was hesitant for several months to really tell outsiders that I had a problem and that I was not drinking. First, I really was not sure if it would stick, that I would be able to maintain total sobriety. I also did not want to answer questions that felt too intrusive about why I was not drinking. Some people are completely open with their struggles. As a Functional in financial services and a female leader, I did not feel comfortable with my information being public. After all, I had worked incredibly hard obtaining my college degree and MBA as well as passing multiple security licenses and gone through years of experience to own my perch in the world. I did not want anything to be taken away from me.

The question of whether to be public about not drinking should be your own. The focus should be on getting yourself better and sorted out. You do not owe anyone an explanation. It can be extremely healthy to be anonymous, especially at first since you are still figuring it all out. I cocooned myself like a caterpillar in this new sober world, testing out what I thought about it. By doing that, I kept myself safe and comfortable with other people in recovery.

As months went by, my mind changed on the topic of being anonymous. First, I witnessed people being public about being alcohol-free or stating

Functional

that they were a year sober, and if they did this on social media, all they received on their Facebook or Instagram pages was love and support from friends and family. These people would tell me that privately they received messages from friends asking for help either for themselves or a family member. While addiction feels like a deeply personal problem, there are so many people who struggle with drinking too much, and every person in this world has a friend, brother, parent, cousin, or coworker who has had issues with drinking.

Second, my mind changed because *I* changed. I was happy naturally without any mind-altering substances. I felt like myself and proud to walk around in my skin. I thought that if sobriety were a pill you could take, you would want to scream from the rooftops about its benefits. I was sleeping like a baby, I was saving money, and the terrible blackouts had stopped. My relationship with my husband had improved and I was killing it at work. Even my appearance improved. If any pharmaceutical drug could offer those benefits, it would be the most successful pill in history and here I found it just from giving up alcohol.

Also, the people I surrounded myself with influenced my thinking. Previously, I was hanging out with self-described "winos" and others who drank a lot. My friend group changed, and I was now surrounded by people who were transforming themselves and were in the process of getting better or had at least somewhat "arrived" at being alcohol-free. In addition, people in recovery are some of the most incredible human beings you will ever meet, and I really did not want to be private about those relationships. I had plenty of friends who'd stopped drinking and then started again and were trying to get better. In contrast, I recognized I was lucky so far: I was maintaining my day count without drinking or relapsing. All those friends who struggled continued to tell me repeatedly that the drink wasn't worth it. I remember when White Claw, the hard seltzer, came out. With its slim drink profile and pop of color for flavor representation, the thought of drinking a White Claw danced in my brain. It would be a fun summer drink to have, and I felt sorrow that I had decided to become alcohol-free before I had a chance to drink "the White Claw."

I was telling a group of recovery people about this desire, and there was a guy who told me he relapsed after five months sober on White Claw because he too was curious and wanted to experience it. Echoing others, he told me it was not worth it, and he would have had over a year sober if he had not drunk it and spun out drinking hard for two months afterward. He looked regretful and like he had lost something significant. I told him that I truly needed to hear that and my little fantasies about White Claw quickly left my imagination.

I was first out on Instagram, because it is a social media platform where more of my friends are than Facebook. That said, I have many more "friends" on Facebook than Instagram. On Instagram, I have a profile that identifies myself as alcohol-free. I have listed a few of my sober birthdays, most notably when I turned two years sober. On Facebook, I have friends who are my relatives, my mom's friends, and most frighteningly, my coworkers. I have not been "out" on Facebook as I write this, simply because I don't feel like I have that many true friends on Facebook and that they are more acquaintances. It also invites questions that I just don't feel like answering. If you are a work colleague and we are connected, would they ask if I drank at work? (I did not and was super controlled at any work functions that required drinking for fear my secret would be discovered.)

For years, I would scribble musings into a Google or Word document about being alcohol-free and the beautiful life it has given me, but I never shared it. After I hit five years alcohol-free, I was on a retreat/vacation with these beautiful women who were mostly in recovery, and

Functional

it really hit me that I wanted to author a book about being a Functional and the freedom that being alcohol-free has given me. That freedom had to be expressed publicly. I mean, if you escaped hell and lived to tell about it, shouldn't you be proud and write about it?!

That said, some professions, religions, and cultures have grave stigmas about addiction. If you are a school principal, doctor, psychiatrist, or social worker, there may be consequences to being public about an addiction. To admit a vulnerability can expose you to career risk. If you are a school principal in charge of children, will you behave alcoholically in front of impressionable audiences or be a bad example? It is no surprise that people in certain professions may suffer in silence with addiction issues. Even if you become sober, you may not be public with that sobriety, because it calls into question your moral character. Personally, I was pretty quiet about my issue for years, even when I became sober, at least at first. I did not want my career or leadership that I had worked so hard for to be scrutinized. At over six years sober, I am more confident in my decision to not drink and feel more comfortable about being publicly alcohol-free.

There are people who publicly announced they were "now sober" exceedingly early in sobriety, and this was very successful for them. They loudly drove a stake in the ground, and it helped them stay away from people, places, and things that would wreck their sobriety. I remember hearing someone at work coming back from rehab and stating, "I'm sober now and going out and being at a bar is hard right now, so I am going to pass on the team happy hour." When they said that, the group knew they were receiving an authentic response from this person and boundaries were established and respected. In contrast, I have had drinks put into my hand by nice, unsuspecting people when I was early in sobriety. I was not out about being sober, so it was not their fault. I put those drinks down immediately on a nearby table, but I did not correct those who gave them to me or tell people I did not drink anymore. I remember being over two years sober and someone I had not seen in a long time sent me a huge wine glass meme about being drunk. I was so irritated with this person, but had to stop myself because they couldn't have known that I no longer drank. So, there is a lesson here: it may not be the best approach for you to be anonymous.

You need to figure out where you are in the process. When you stop drinking, you become more of who you are meant to be and find what makes YOU comfortable.

Some questions to ask yourself:

- *Does it make you uncomfortable to tell people that you do not drink?*

- *What words FEEL right to describe you? I like to tell people that I am alcohol-free, because it FEELS empowering to be free of an addictive substance and it is a positive association. Sometimes, I say that I am sober. Those identifications ring true to me. What words ring true to you?*

- *If you are not out publicly about not drinking, is there any one person with whom you can be authentic? My husband is a person I tell my struggles to, and he was someone that I could talk to initially about my experiment of not drinking. I also could tell him about books or podcasts I was listening to when I was first not drinking, and he would listen to me and ask questions. Do you have someone like that, such as a friend, parent, partner, or coworker?*

Spouses, Partners, and Significant Others

Changing your relationship to drinking is mostly a singular endeavor. After all, only you can keep yourself from not drinking. That said, the relationships we have in our lives are profoundly influenced by those we love and are surrounded by on a regular basis. For most people, our spouse, partner, or closest friend is a cherished and important person, and we share households, money, and key life experiences. If we decide to give up drinking, it impacts those relationships. There are multiple dynamics that exist that I will discuss, such as the parallel situation of a significant other who is your "drinking buddy" and drinks about the same as you, or a relationship where you are the heavy drinker and your spouse drinks less or not at all. In general, you know if your partner drinks more or less than you. If they drink more, they may regret you not drinking. If they drink less, they may be excited for you to quit.

For my situation, I had the latter: My husband hardly drank. In fact, my biggest guilt in my drinking was around my husband. When we married, I was not a problem drinker, and it just was not an issue. In a lot of ways, my husband is a strong partner for me. Like me, he is industrious and a hard worker and respects order and structure. We both are planners and think about the future. Also, we share a soft spot for animals, and we have taken in a few strays and adopted another from the Humane Society. That said, all the parties and gatherings in our home that we hosted had alcohol; I was a good host, and we were always stocked. As I drank daily and it was not just social anymore, it became a concern, and we increasingly fought about the amount I drank.

For him, it was "Rachel, can't you just have one or two drinks?!" Of course, I was blowing past those limits and having only one drink was torture. He really did not understand ruining your next day with drinking from the night before and his hobbies never involved drinking. My hobbies involved going out to new restaurants and wineries, and all my girlfriends were "the winos." He loves to work on cars and that is not a hobby where you typically drink, or you may lose a digit. My drinking was causing a problem, especially because our drinking patterns were different.

My husband was incredibly supportive when I quit drinking. I started attending AA and other online recovery meetings and told him about what I was learning about alcohol as a toxic substance and how I was questioning why I drank and what triggered me. I remember during my first month, he checked on me and asked how I was doing without drinking. I would tell him my day count such as "Day 10" and he would tell me "Good job, Rachel." We also both love praise, and I appreciated his encouragement and support. I asked him to attend an open AA meeting with me, so he could understand what it was like and hear the new people and program that I was experiencing. The open AA meeting was in an urban environment, which was slightly uncomfortable for my straitlaced, country-raised husband.

I remember that the large meeting was led by a theatrical man in a vampire cape and punk haircut, and my husband attended and gave me a quizzical look at some of the verbiage and dramatics of the speaker.

Functional

That said, he was supportive: He would tell me that he liked my laugh more now that I was sober because it sounded real and more authentic. He would listen to me when I was worried about attending an event where there would be a lot of drinking. He told me often he was proud of me. He was never much of a drinker before I was sober, but now he rarely drinks. He had one beer in a three-year period. He told me that he could hardly finish it! Of course, I am the main impetus for his lack of drinking, but he just really does not like it and would rather be productive. He has sat at plenty of bars, restaurants, and boozy social events with me drinking sparkling water and it has been a kind of comfort.

The change of being sober has strengthened my marriage and we are more aligned as a couple. For example, we have always done do-it-yourself projects, but we have taken on more advanced home renovations together. He is the 80 percent: putting up fireplace tile, cutting trim and patching sheetrock. I am the 20 percent: picking out paint color, coordinating carpet installers, picking out furniture, creating a design vision as well as a budget. We move through my sobriety with a partnership that just gets deeper. I sleep closer to him at night because my breath does not smell like alcohol, which used to repulse him. In sobriety, we will tackle home projects for a guest bedroom, increased storage for a primary bedroom closet, and even a family room. All these spaces we share, and they will enhance our domestic bliss. Even our cats' lives improved in my sobriety: we built a warm and cozy family room with a new fireplace that my cats sleep in front of during cold Minnesotan nights.

A more common relationship dynamic especially for drinkers is to have a partner who also drinks. You may have first met your significant other in a bar or out drinking with friends or colleagues. If you are used to bonding with your spouse over a drink after a long day at work, you may think that your full relationship is entwined with drinking, and you can go through a "double breakup" with booze and then your partner. In this situation, you may need extra support from sober circles because you may feel lonelier, and I would encourage you to obtain that support. In addition, you may need to communicate and enforce your needs, such as keeping alcohol out of the house so you are not tempted to drink or skipping out on an event with too much alcohol.

Another support that you may need from your partner is time away to focus on sobriety, such as meeting with other sober people or attending a retreat. Plenty of people in my online community have time during the day when they attend a meeting, and family members know that this time is off-limits and not to bother them, similar to a work meeting. Perhaps, you need a retreat or in-person rehab that your partner will have to consider or take care of the children while you are away. It may mean juggling schedules, child pickup duties and taking care of household responsibilities, such as mowing the lawn or paying the bills. As Functionals, we will want to keep our lives intact, and you may need to work out these details with your partner or even ask for additional support from your parents, friends, or hire help. It could be temporary or longer but set yourself up for success. A regular, in-person meeting for one hour a week could be the difference between you drinking and making everyone's life more difficult. Reframing the small sacrifice that a partner may have to make to support you can help everyone understand the priority. This can be especially helpful for someone who has a partner who drinks, and they may especially need support and community with others who do not drink.

It is no secret that if you stop drinking and your partner continues to drink a lot that it may cause friction in your relationship. The stakes are higher with the relationship especially if you are married, share property, or children/pets. There is specific advice in the rooms of AA to not make big decisions such as a divorce in the first year that you give up drinking, because you want to be certain and level out your life before making major changes. I have seen couples both change to become sober, or one partner significantly lowers their drinking intake when another gets sober. It's a life improvement, and your significant other may be on board for that change, especially if you model positivity. That said, there are relationships that end when one partner gets sober.

Finally, you could have a spouse or partner who has a more neutral or moderate response. Perhaps, they drink, but not a lot. Even my husband, who rarely drank, wondered how it would work if we went on vacation at all-inclusive resorts, since that was something we both liked. Like a new job or new home, there can be an adjustment period when you change a key habit. It can take a minute to be in sync with not only your partner, but also yourself. You may just need time to experience your new self in your relationship to figure out how it will work. With the issue of the all-inclusive resorts, my husband and I discovered that we actually prefer renting out a house with a pool all to ourselves with snacks and sparkling water that we buy at a supermarket, instead of paying outrageous prices for lackluster buffets and liquor that we no longer drink.

Questions to ask yourself:

- *How do you think your relationship will be like after you take a break or stop drinking?*
- *Do you think that your partner's viewpoint on drinking is fixed or can be changed?*
- *Regardless of how they feel, how can you take care of yourself? Is there any request that you can make of your partner to help you be more successful?*

Friend Groups

What if your issue is your friends or your best friend are drinkers and that is how you are accustomed to bonding and socializing with them? What if you have several great memories of happy hours, weddings, or "emergency" bar bonding sessions with close friends where you can commiserate about lousy boyfriends, bad bosses or the injustices of life? All my friends were winos. I had networked my way in business over happy hours and spent my free time exploring cool cocktail bars and wineries with friends. I have invested time, feelings, and friendships in this space. In early sobriety, I did not know if being alcohol-free was a temporary change or permanent change. I wasn't going to just immediately drop these relationships.

I started out by telling my core group of friends that I was going alcohol-free for a month, which was wise in hindsight. A few confessed to me that they wanted to do the same thing ... at some point. It also coincided with another woman becoming pregnant, so now there were two of us who were not drinking. It made the group consider the friendship now that the members were changing.

Functional

One of my friends was extremely supportive and she expressed that to the group in a very public way. She was the admin for our group chat, and she changed our group name from Winos to a name focused on friendship. I appreciated this gesture, especially because I had concert tickets and other planned events that I was doing. We were friends after all.

In my first three to six months, I continued to attend get-togethers with them. That said, it would get more difficult. We were just on different frequencies, and I couldn't ignore that I was on a different path to self-discovery and change. Gradually, we just didn't have as much in common. I would attend events where they would be drinking and after two drinks, it just would not be fun for me anymore. They would be louder, rowdier, and then turn depressive, insecure, and insensitive. This was the alcohol speaking and I believe at the core that they are lovely people. I would increasingly find that I just wanted to spend my time differently, and they likely saw me as a killjoy and changed from how I previously was.

I have run into them individually when I was out or have wished them "Happy Birthday" or "Congrats on the new baby." It's been friendly, but we do not hang out. People change and friendships change. If I go back in time, I don't believe that I would have changed the progression. I needed to experience time with them sober to understand what I wanted from life and friendship.

For what it is worth, I gained a lot more friends after I became sober. They just were not the same friends. There are so many people that I have met who are in recovery or who are not really focused on drinking, and they live a life more in the present moment. I am more content with friendships now.

Friend Groups

I included this section because friendship can be a gray area. After all, these are not your romantic partners, but relationships still matter and navigating it can be tricky. I would trust the process and your new sober compass. If the relationship doesn't feel the same or if being in an environment with them doesn't feel good, leave or find a way out of it. In addition, it is likely that the same group of people with whom you drank may have issues with alcohol that could be like yours. I have been sober for over six years and a few of those same friends have reached out to me because they have struggled with their relationship with drinking. They may not understand it initially, but they will recognize and respect boundaries.

Slips and Relapses

During COVID, which was one of the most difficult times for all humans in the world, there were some sober people I know who relapsed. There was so much change and uncertainty about the world: The virus was not treatable, and the world shut down. The only places that seemed to be open were grocery and liquor stores. Parents had to homeschool and we were suddenly all on Zoom calls staring at small squares, living with all our noisy family members and pets and trying to work. The COVID cocktail, the "Quarantini," a take on the classic martini, became an overnight sensation. There was so much change and stress, why not drink?! We were all stuck at home and didn't have to go into an office. Would anyone REALLY know if the coffee cup mug had vodka in it?

As I write this chapter, we are still in COVID. We are twenty-one days away from the end of a divisive election. There has been ample civil unrest and racial reckoning. I also live twenty minutes away from Minneapolis. I worked in Minneapolis every day and have lived in Minneapolis or near it my whole life. I will never forget the George Floyd protests or the subsequent days when my city was under curfew for about a week, because of the fires, rioting, and civil unrest. It is

Slips and Relapses

incredibly sad and disquieting to hear people chanting "Burn it down" and see your home city up in flames.

In some ways, it has been a beautiful year, but it has also been a very tough year. Because it has been a tough year, a few people in my recovery circle have relapsed. They had longer than a year in recovery. I looked up to them and held them to higher standards. I drew strength from them and modeled their sobriety as what I wanted in my life.

Relapse is understandable. Drinking was my habit and solved (poorly and momentarily) my problems. Drinking was an ingrained habit. Every time I drank, I convinced my body and mind that alcohol was the solution to my discontent. Also, alcohol is everywhere: All restaurants have it on the menu, many people drink, and I am of legal age to walk into a liquor store and purchase it. If I want it, I can get it. Sometimes, staying sober can feel like an impossible goal. I get that. Still, it disappoints me when someone relapses, because one may not come back after it, and I have never witnessed a case when it gets better. I will say it again: I have never seen someone who has a problem with alcohol, stop, and drink again and have it not be painful and a problem.

Within the sobriety world, people view this topic differently. I like all the viewpoints, and they all provide a healthy perspective. In AA, when you drink again after you begin this sober journey, it would be called a relapse. In AA, this does mean that you restart your "clock" on Day 1. I would say that there is only love for people who come back and humbly admit that they are on Day 1 again. There are plenty of people who have gone to meetings for years or who came in and out of the program, and people understand.

There is also the Smart Recovery concept where someone drinks, but they may not get drunk or abuse alcohol. Smart recovery calls it a "slip." The way they see it is that this is not total devastation and a person with this

Functional

problem can "get back on the horse" and continue an alcohol-free life. I like both the concepts of the slip and the relapse. I think being sober is the way to go, but I do not believe that we should be so hard on ourselves when we are trying to get sober, especially in the beginning. This is a whole new world and becoming a new person with new habits is ridiculously hard at first. A person who used to get drunk every day for years, stops, then has a day or two of drinking is still an improvement over the previous cycle. Better is better. If you have a six-month period where you drank three days, that is 177 days out of 180 days sober, or a 98.3 percent success rate. By any measurement, we would say that it is successful, especially if someone was drinking more often than that in the past.

That said, slips and relapses may not be a "light" or moderate event. It can mean death, harm to others, or never getting back to sober days again. I do see a trend of people who are trying to be alcohol-free and have some time under their belt trying drinking again. Because alcohol is a toxin and depressant, they recognize how bad they feel and normally report that the drink "wasn't worth it," especially if they are used to productive mornings and not feeling anxious.

I have a unique beginning. I started this whole thing by trying for a sober September and I was only going to commit to a month. I just kept going because I knew being alcohol-free was working. Most people I meet do not have such a simple, black-and-white path. They stop drinking. They start drinking. They stop for a period of time. They think they have "learned therapeutic skills" or dealt with problems and they think they can drink again. Sometimes, whatever they are dealing with in their life just becomes too much and they go back to their old friend alcohol.

Or sometimes, 2020 happens and you lose a stable job, or you must homeschool your kid for months on end and you drink again. 2020 was a tough year for alcoholics. All Americans were drinking more.

Slips and Relapses

According to Nielsen's market data, total alcohol sales outside of bars and restaurants surged 24 percent during the pandemic. Sales of spirits with higher alcohol content rose even faster, a more than 27 percent increase over the previous year (Source: Hangover From Alcohol Boom Could Last Long After Pandemic Ends | npr.org).

It was influential for me to have a first sponsor who relapsed after having about six years of sobriety under her belt and came back. She had been sober for several years when she sponsored me. She is a cool lady and told me a drink will never taste the same after you go back and all her behaviors and problems eventually returned after she went back to drinking. She did not lecture and was pretty matter of fact about her relapse experience. Eventually, I would meet people who "went back out," which is the term used when people went back to drinking. Every time, my curious brain wanted to hear a story or a single instance where someone could successfully moderate after they took a break.

But I never met someone who convinced me that their lives were better by returning to alcohol. Never ever, and I REALLY wanted to meet those people, especially when I first stopped, because I did want to see if I could successfully moderate. I had friends who went back out and gradually drank, only to end up drinking to the same elevated level that they had previously and clawing their way back to getting sober days. I had friends who went back to drinking and hit a new bottom like losing their job. I had a friend who was a year sober go back out and find his depression again and end up killing himself while drunk. Sure, I had examples of people who started drinking again and they told me that it "was not like before" when they threw up in Ubers or partied like they used to. That said their drinking would start with a glass or two and end up ramping up and just go back to an unmanageable level. I just could not find a long-term example where returning to the substance led to a better place than simply not drinking.

Functional

I have always found positivity in people who come back from a relapse. A longtime publicly sober guy, Dax Shepard, relapsed in October 2020. Dax had been sober from alcohol and cocaine for sixteen years and still is sober from these previous drugs. He relapsed on prescription drugs, something that started from his motorsports crashes and grew into him hiding his use and admitting on a podcast that he was not sober from prescription drugs and decided to reset his counter. He created a Day 7 podcast episode where he admitted to his listeners his problem and how he put his friend and fellow podcast host in a terrible place by stealing pills that he had made her responsible for giving to him at certain times. He talked about being a very public person in recovery with a famous wife and how he felt like a fraud celebrating a soberversary cake with people in AA, while he knew that he was abusing pills. It was an excellent episode because it touched on relapsing and learning to change. He also talked about how he went back to his AA community, and they welcomed him with open arms and support.

When I listen to episodes like that, it reminds me just how crazy drugs and alcohol can make us. The lying, the hiding, the deception with the people we love make me sick: All the shameful aspects about addiction are revealed. That said, I do believe you learn when you relapse. When I was newly sober, I used to be really scared about relapsing. You just do not feel strong, and you recognize how attractive alcohol can look. Many people talk about the dreaded drinking dreams, where you drink in your dreams and you go back to lying, doing things that you would never do when you are sober, and then wake up in a pool of sweat realizing that it was all a dream. Once you are conscious, you realize that it was "just a dream" and you have no alcohol taste in your mouth and your brain is not foggy. Those drinking dreams always convinced me of a saying that I have heard in the rooms, which is "There are more drinks left in me, but not another recovery." Yes, I may dream about drinking, but could I come back from it? It was so difficult to get sober and stay sober initially. Now, I rarely ever think about drinking and before it used to consume me. I just can't go back, and I really don't want to, especially if I have dreams of drinking.

At the two-year sobriety mark, something shifted in me. And now I totally recognize that being alcohol-free is without a doubt the best life for me. All these amazing things happened to me when I gave up the substance that was secretly enslaving me. I had this realization that even if I were to go back to drinking, I would have had enough sober days to KNOW that being alcohol-free is better. I also had good tools and resources if I were to get in a bad place again. I could go any time of day to a meeting. I could message a friend in my recovery circle. I really did have options.

Also, when I did my daily practices like writing my gratitude list in my five-minute journal or completing my morning pages, I realized that I had habits that were ensuring my sobriety. When I put myself to bed early because my body was too tired, I was also ensuring my sobriety. When I saw beauty in the world and took myself to a flower shop to buy a beautiful bouquet of fresh flowers instead of buying a "nice bottle of wine," I was also feeding my sobriety soul.

As a final thought: When you are in rooms of recovery, there is a saying that it is easier to STAY sober instead of trying to GET sober. The cycle of drinking, recovering from drinking, and feeling bad mentally and physically afterward is more painful than just staying sober and having to deal with new feelings. That cycle is exhausting and full of shame. I tried to moderate, and it just wasn't helpful, because I couldn't ultimately reach a destination, and I didn't ultimately trust myself. I have a friend who has incredible diligence in eating well and going to a very tough yoga class on a nearly daily basis, but she is having the most difficult time staying sober even after multiple rehab stays. She is embarrassed that "she can't get it" and she is stuck in a cycle, and it is tough to see her suffer. In contrast, those with longer sobriety represent themselves more confidently, their relationships and employment are secure, and they rarely think about drinking.

Pain

"I've never seen any life transformation that didn't begin with the person in question finally getting tired of their own bullshit." — Elizabeth Gilbert

With drinking, we have taught ourselves to numb our pain. A Functional uses a socially appropriate way to numb such as the idea of "a drink" that rewards us for a grueling day of work. In contrast, we understand that a paper bag bottle of hard liquor would make us look like a bum under a bridge. It would be uncouth for a Functional with a decent job, family, and good social standing to engage in hard drugs and likely it would never cross our mind. Yet, we seek out a substance such as alcohol to minimize the daily pain that we endure to keep it all together.

There is another side to pain in recovery. Bob Dylan once said, "Behind every beautiful thing, there been some kind of pain." Babies that come from women's bodies are miraculous occurrences, but they require pain. Sprouts that burst from the ground to develop into healthy plants require pain. Homes that are constructed by tradesmen through digging out a foundation, raising construction beams, and running electrical wires carefully through multiple levels and rooms require painstaking work. Wars that are bravely fought with loss of lives and sacrifice at home require pain to get to and protect freedom. Intuitively, we know that all great transformation stories to create things that truly matter will involve a change that was in some way painful and hard.

The process of living an alcohol-free life, at least initially deals with pain. While pain is a natural part of life and inevitable, you will have to brace yourself for some discomfort. Pain may look like: sitting through a craving. Telling someone uncomfortably that you do not drink. Pain may be missing the sense of connection that one had with drinking that with a partner or friend. Dealing with pain in recovery may look like taking a walk after a stressful day at work instead of heading to the bar. It may be a little painful and you may suffer some personal pride in telling someone that you need help instead of keeping silent.

To deal with pain, sometimes we must use motivation techniques to get us through the pain. When I heard that cravings only last twenty minutes, I remember telling myself this repeatedly to remind myself that it was a fleeting period and that I was on a countdown to feeling normal. I would distract myself in that twenty-minute period. I would clean, scroll social media, or go to the mailbox. Inevitably, I would be distracted from the pain and forget about it. It was annoying and hard at first, but increasingly, I could get through the pain until it just was not there anymore.

Sometimes I went to a meeting and complained about the "new" pain, which was recovering. To a group of people all suffering from the same problem, I would say I wanted wine to deal with the stupid person at work who made me want to drink. I would say that I was sick of watching all the damn alcohol ads on TV that I could not escape. I would tell the group that I just needed to last through my niece's birthday where glasses of rosé would be served. The group would listen, and we would

Functional

commiserate and solve together and inevitably I would hear what I needed to hear to get through the pain. There was another aspect of sharing pain with others: I felt less lonely and there was relief in the share. Occasionally, I would have people come up to me afterward and say they felt something similar, especially when I was trying to figure out how to operate in the world without my drug of choice. Those conversations soothed me in a healthier way than drinking ever could.

On the topic of pain, it is important to mention that drinking is also very painful. The genuinely surprising and shocking thing to me was that drinking was much more painful than stopping, especially after I used many of the tools. Headaches, mood swings, the day-after anxiety, stomachaches, diarrhea, telling lies about how much you drank, not remembering the texts that you sent, and especially not living up to your potential are all pretty painful. The terrible aspect about this is we are Functional and on a fundamental level we understand we are failing. Failing is the long-term hangover, and that is very, very painful indeed.

Choose your pain. Life will always be painful, but being alcohol-free for me has been about freedom and confidence, and all the rest of the temporary pain that came with it has been worth it. I hope by writing this book I have provided the reader with reliable information and tools and resources for a different, healthier path, and I wish you all luck.

Final Chapter: Contrast Your Drinking Self with Your Alcohol-Free Self

To maintain our preferred drinking habits while also being productive members of society, Functionals are adept at balancing two different realities. This means that we think we can manage in both environments, at least temporarily, and in some cases, for quite some time. Once I felt like I'd figured out this alcohol-free lifestyle, I often reflected on what I would have told my drinking self about what it was like to be alcohol-free as well as the process of learning to stay that way. I had all kinds of preconceptions and *frankly* misconceptions about what would happen.

This is a fictional account of myself split into two Rachels: The Rachel who used to drink pre-2018 (Drinking Rachel) and me in present time (Sober Rachel).

Drinking Rachel: *Expertly corks the wine bottle and pours herself a tall glass of pinot grigio.* OK, now that I have my drink, I can focus on this conversation. So, you *actually* did it? You stopped drinking for more than three days without cheating? Is that *true*? You must have been miserable? Did you have bad withdrawal? Was it the worst thing that you had ever experienced?

Functional

Sober Rachel: *Opens a can of watermelon sparkling water and takes a sip.* Yeah, I really did it. Today, I have been sober for over six years and most of the time, it feels incredible. I did stop drinking and never went back—knock on wood. There were times when I binged on chocolate chip cookies and Netflix and hid from the world, but I did not drink. It is remarkable and it has made me open to miracles.

As far as being miserable and having bad withdrawals, that did not happen. I can honestly tell you I had night sweats around Day 3, weird dreams, and some intense cravings (that went away), but nothing has been as bad as those terrible hangovers—you know what I mean, Rachel. In fact, in hindsight, there might be nothing as bad as a hangover. The shaking, the nausea, the headaches, the diarrhea, and the disgusting taste in my mouth. Ugh, that really sucked.

Drinking Rachel: Six whole years, huh? That is pretty impressive. Where did I go? I cannot even imagine. *She studies the glowing liquid of her glass, and the next question has an edge of snarkiness to it:* So, are you one of those super boring people, now? I do not mean to be rude, but not drinking, or "alcohol-free" as you call it, sounds so ... boring. Do you just stay home and do nothing and have no friends now that you do not drink?

Sober Rachel: Actually, it is just the opposite. Let's face it, it is pretty boring to get blasted every night and be a blob at work the next day and into the next evening. You were unremarkable and predictable. You went to work, came home, drank. Rinse and repeat. Even when you worked out on days after you drank, you still never gave it your all!

When you first stop drinking, you will have an insane amount of energy, and you will feel like you are about seven years younger. Fountain of youth. Really.

Final Chapter: Contrast Your Drinking Self with Your Alcohol-Free Self

As far as the friends, here is what will happen: You will lose friends you drank with, and you will be a little sad about that. You will miss them. That said, you will get this whole new set of friends and acquaintances that you never, ever saw coming. They will be interesting, and you will have an immediate and authentic connection. You will travel with them a whole lot, and they will cheer you on. You will have some of the best dinners and discussions on a beach that you have ever had. In terms of actual friend numbers, your friends will increase threefold. You will genuinely be surprised at how easy it can be to make friends, even as an adult in your forties.

Sometimes, you will stay at home, but your home is going to get better. Really, you will be blown away by where you end up living. It will be quite unexpected. You will eventually move to a beautiful location in the country and your views of nature will be expansive and serene. You will see active wildlife as you sit on a covered porch and watch big, white puffy clouds move across the sky. You will also encounter new animals and end up owning pets that will delight you that you will hold dear. It will be nothing like you can imagine now but trust me it is particularly good.

Drinking Rachel: *A little interested, but unconvinced.* Yeah, OK, so what about work? How will you make it through a business dinner or happy hour without drinking? Won't everyone expect you to share a bottle of wine?

Sober Rachel: You are going to be uncomfortable at first when it comes to interacting with people professionally without drinking. But you will figure it all out. You will also be surprised how many people do not drink, and you will be even more surprised at how many people do not care what you drink. In addition, you will find that people change after a few drinks and may compromise themselves or their company. I will

Functional

tell you something that will really motivate you: Sober Rachel will be a powerhouse professionally and kill it at work. By not drinking, you will impress the right people, you will advance quickly, and you will be surprised how easy that more complex work will become once you stop drinking. You will sense when people are bullshitting you. You also will become a lot more confident and take on larger responsibilities and with that, increased salary and bonuses.

Drinking Rachel: *Pours herself more from the bottle of pinot grigio with flushed cheeks. She is getting braver and decides to be more candid in her questions.* Well, I can see that you look better and a little slimmer. Is it just me or do you not look puffy?! Did the money you make go toward more Botox and a good nutritionist or something? And let us be honest here: Is sex actually any fun without a buzz?

Sober Rachel: *Chokes a little on her sparkling water.* I forgot how direct you can be when you've had a little liquid courage. OK, let us take the questions one by one. First, I look better because I do not have a toxic substance pulsing through my body, and I get quality sleep. Rachel, the sleep you will get is delicious and something that will blow you away. You will still need Botox from time to time, because you do age after all, but that weird rash you had on your chest will go away and your eyes will be that bright blue again, like when you were a child.

You will not need a dietician because you will instantly lose a few pounds when you go out of the hooch. The crazy thing you will find out is that food flavors are incredible after you give up alcohol, because alcohol dulls your taste buds. So, you will feel more satisfied with the food, and you will rarely have to diet. You will never weigh as much as you did when you were drinking. Let me say it differently: wine makes you heavier and you will maintain your weight easier without drinking.

As for the sex question, it is yet another thing that is better without drinking. First, you will remember everything afterward and you will

Final Chapter: Contrast Your Drinking Self with Your Alcohol-Free Self

be more in tune with what you want. It just IS better because you can feel it and you will not be numb and mindless when it happens. Although you already know this, your husband will find you much more attractive without drinking as well and you both will genuinely connect more easily.

Drinking Rachel: *Slurring a little...* Real question, Rachel. How did you deal with the stress and all the rumination? You know what I mean—drinking seemed to be the only way to stop all that overthinking. Did all of that just go away suddenly or what? How did you figure out how to sleep at night without wine?!

Sober Rachel: *Looks straight at Drinking Rachel:* That never truly went away and if anything, the stress intensified, especially as I moved up the ranks professionally. When you put down the alcohol and stop using it as a solution, you can use other mechanisms to cope. You will have support groups that you will rely on, and you will also have some surprising mentors and sponsors. These were tools that you never utilized prior.

You will fall in love with baths that will help you sleep. That said, your sleep will come back naturally after you figure out that all the booze was causing you to sleep like crap. Finally, you will eventually own a country home that is a calm sanctuary, and you will really sleep well there. The 3 a.m. anxiety attacks of hangiexty and shame will cease, and you will feel surprisingly good about yourself. Your sleeplessness never goes away completely, but it is significantly better.

The worry and rumination never totally leave, but they are manageable. They become a useful ability in corporate America, because they help you solve problems. On an instinctive level, you already know that and use that rumination. That said, it just becomes healthier and not as consumable once you stop drinking.

Functional

Drinking Rachel looks unconvinced, and her eyes are half shut now. She can't seem to focus on what you are saying and looks like she just wants to nod off and sleep.

Sober Rachel: Let's revisit this conversation once you have sobered up tomorrow.

Today, if I could say one final thing to Drinking Rachel-and to anyone that recognizes themselves in her-it would be this: the life that you are so afraid of is possible and it is waiting for you. I once thought that alcohol gave me rest, connection, and relieved my anxiety. In reality, it was an unfulfilled promise that gradually deprived me of those things. Once I stopped drinking, a richer and more satisfying life emerged-one that I never could have imagined when I was still under alcohol's spell.

Humans are not meant to live split lives, constantly battling between the person that we want to be and the addictions holding us back. We are meant to live whole and authentic lives. If you are standing once where I stood, doubting that change is possible or if your life is not "bad enough", I hope this book shows you that it is not only possible-it is better than you can possibly imagine. You have all the willpower, strength, and inner knowledge inside of you. Trust yourself enough to find out who you are without alcohol. I promise you won't regret meeting the real you.

Recommended Resources
(in no particular order)

Books

We are the Luckiest: The Surprising Magic of a Sober Life
Laura McKowen

Quit Like a Woman
Holly Whitaker

This Naked Mind: Transform your life and empower yourself to drink less or even quit alcohol with this practical how-to guide rooted in science to boost your wellbeing
Annie Grace

Nothing Good Can Come from This
Kristi Coulter

She Recovers Every Day
Dawn Nickel

Sober Lush: A Hedonist's Guide to Living a Decadent, Adventurous, Soulful Life-Alcohol-Free
Amanda Eyre Ward

The Unexpected Joy of Being Sober: Discovering a Happy, Healthy, Wealthy Alcohol-Free Life
Catherine Gray

Alcoholics Anonymous: The Story of How More Than One Hundred Men Have Recovered from Alcoholism (nicknamed The Big Book)
Bill W.

Functional

Drink: The Intimate Relationship Between Woman and Alcohol
Ann Dowsett Johnston

The Woman's Way Through the Twelve Steps
Stephanie S. Covington

Podcasts

- Recovery Elevator
- We Can Do Hard Things
- Home
- This Naked Mind
- The One You Feed
- Unruffled
- Armchair Expert (not a sole recovery podcast, but the host and several guests are in recovery)
- Editing our drinking and our lives with Jolene Park and Donnelley Rowley
- Recovery Happy Hour with Tricia Lewis
- SheRecovers

Support groups

- The Luckiest Club
- Alcoholics Anonymous
- Smart Recovery
- SheRecovers
- Recovery Elevator
- Monument

Final Chapter: Contrast Your Drinking Self with Your Alcohol-Free Self

Sober Instagram people to follow

- Laura McKowen
- My Kind of Sweet
- Euphoric
- Sober Mom Squad
- My Badass Recovery
- Sober Girls Society
- Sober.Powered

Made in the USA
Middletown, DE
01 June 2025